The Lure of Gems
An Encyclopaedic Guide
Volume I

By Steve Bennett

INTRODUCTION TO
VOLUME I

Welcome to volume one of "The Lure of Gems": an encyclopaedic reference guide to gemstones and jewellery.

I really hope you find this encyclopaedia useful and informative. There are two reasons why I have split this book into two volumes: firstly, as most customers will be receiving this book by post, the weight of a book over one thousand pages thick would push up the delivery cost, but secondly and most importantly it is taking me so long to write this book in-between running my main business Gems TV that quite frankly I have yet to finish writing the entire works! There is every chance that as you read this book, if the second volume has not yet been published, then I am somewhere in the world, possibly in some remote mining location typing up the next volume on my iPad.

I hope you like the content and the layout and as always I welcome any feedback.

Welcome to the world of Mother Nature's treasures: a world full of colourful locations, colourful people, colourful stories and, of course - colourful gems.

HOW TO USE THIS
A TO Z BOOK

"The Lure of Gems" has been written in an A to Z encyclopaedic format, so that you can dip in and out at your leisure. Whenever you come across a new gemstone or hear someone mention a jewellery term that you have not heard before, you can easily use the book's A to Z format to quickly find out more.

In keeping with the encylopaedic format, we have not always explained a term every time it is used (otherwise this book would run into two thousand pages). Instead, we have kept repetition to a minimum in the knowledge that you will be able to cross-reference other sections of this book if you encounter any unfamiliar terms.

THANKS

I would like to start by saying a huge thank you and lots of love to our chief jewellery designer, my wife, who worked many hours guiding my research on the history of jewellery.

A big thank you must go to my eldest daughter Hannah: many of her illustrations, in particular her drawings of the Crown Jewels are amazingly accurate. Also a big thanks to my eldest son Matt who accompanies me on most of my gem adventures around the globe; many of the on location photos in this book are taken by him (well, the better ones anyway).

Many thanks to Glenn Lehrer for your constant mentoring: your help and expertise is always appreciated. Many thanks to Terry Coldham and Paul Sedawin for supplying several photos from Down Under. I am grateful to Rob Gessner of Gemfields for letting me use several of his photographs that were taken during my trip to Zambia in 2010. I also wish to thank my good friend Andy Lucas of the GIA for letting me use some of his photos for the write up on Afghanistan and to Constantine for sending me photos of his home town of Idar-Obestein.

I must not forget a mention to my six children, Hannah, Matt, Jack, Jessica, Tom and Lili, all of whom haven't seen too much of their Dad recently.

A huge thank you to Phil, Dionne, Melissa, Sian, John (my brother) and Brendan, who are the marketing team and the editing team at Gems TV for putting together and laying out this new issue.

Huge thanks to Suzanne Martinez of Lang Antiques Jewellers of San Francisco; most of the photographs under the heading of Art Nouveau and Art Deco are supplied by Suzanne. If you are ever looking to purchase antique jewellery then her website www.langantiques.com is one of the finest in the world and her service and authenticity is second to none.

I would like to also thank the many mine owners who have not only shown me around their mines, but also taken the time to explain in great detail their operations. Huge thanks also to my good friend Manuj Goyal for your ongoing support and continual innovation: it is your vision, work ethics and inspiration that have been a major driving force behind this third issue.

Finally, a massive thanks to the whole team for making it a really enjoyable project. I hope you will get as much pleasure from reading it as we did from writing and designing it.

Preface by the Author Steve Bennett

At 4,000 metres above sea level, in deep dark jungles, in snow-capped mountains, in barren valleys, the vast majority of the world's most precious gemstones are hidden from man in some of the most inhospitable places on Earth. The Khyber Pass, the frozen landscapes of Siberia, the Himalayas, the dusty Aboriginal outback of Australia, the swamps of Madagascar, the forests of Laos: why are these sprinklings of treasures not unearthed in towns and cities of the Western World? Why, if we invest enough time tending to our gardens don't we just occasionally discover a mineral with colours mirroring the flowers we are growing?

The vast majority of the world's coloured gemstones are mined in Third World countries and most are in obscure locations. A fairly safe educated guess would be that over 90% of the coloured gemstones you will ever wear will have been dug out of the ground by an artisanal miner or at most a very small group of individuals. Over the past few years I have visited gemstone mines in such countries as Thailand, India, Zambia, Brazil and Madagascar: even in these countries gemstone mining does not take place in the big cities, but appears to be restricted to inhospitable areas where man would not normally choose to settle.

For me the only logical conclusion as to why gems are discovered where they are, is that God decided He would try and distribute wealth, hope and opportunity for man all across the planet. He must have thought that people born in areas where man supplies, fresh water, flat lands and rivers to provide easy transport, didn't need to have an additional income from His coloured treasures. Instead, He sprinkled them randomly in remote areas, where indigenous people could later uncover them, providing happiness through their beauty, whilst at the same time giving those cut off from society something mystical to believe in. But other than Diamonds, His only gem creation made from just one element, He did not place big pockets of coloured gemstones in organised and logical patterns, but sprinkled them thinly and randomly.

Was His logic behind first choosing inhospitable places and then secondly only sprinkling gems thinly, to ring-fence the income from these coloured stones for locals, understanding that big corporations and large companies would find it difficult to attempt to amass large profits over such a wide area?

For those of us who collect gemstones, our passion and excitement is delivered primarily from studying the beauty of these natural wonders. Many say that it is the rarity that gets us all a little over excited at times, but whilst this does of course influence our emotions it is not the whole story. After all, if rarity was the whole story then Tsavorite would be more prized than Emeralds, and Rubellite more so than Ruby. Collecting gemstones is about connecting with nature: it's about possessing something that is individual and beautiful. Whilst history, geography, geology and science all play supporting roles in our hobby, it's the unique beauty, the individualistic nature of a gem that causes most gem collectors' pulses to race. In the long term, due to their durability our collections can be passed on to future generations and depending on how big a quantity of the gem variety we have collected is then uncovered in the future, combined with how the demand for it increases or decreases through the knowledge spread by our ever increasingly connected world, it may just increase in value.

For those of us who combine our hobby with our business, I feel we have a duty to the indigenous people from where these treasures are unearthed, to work with them to ensure they benefit from their discoveries. I believe it is important that wherever possible, we allow them to conduct their business in the way that best suits them. Whilst we should encourage ethical and environmentally responsible mining, we must be careful that we don't over burden them with our values and idealistic beliefs. In our highly regulated world, full of red tape and bureaucracy, and often with our ill-advised committee based decision making processes, with unclear agendas and sometimes salary motivated conclusions, who are we to dictate exactly how happy and smiling small Third World villages in inhospitable places manage their livelihood?

Don't get me wrong, as a family man and a father of six, I have very strong ews about ethics and best practices. As a family we also have our own charity which supports communities located near gemstone mines in Africa. In Zambia in particular we are working to build an extension to a rural school, a new medical centre, as well as supporting training in farming techniques, but whilst doing all of this, we have to be mindful that we do not try and push our own beliefs and ideologies.

Whilst it would be great to be able to give to every gemstone buying customer a certificate from an artisanal miner saying that he has mined his gemstone in accordance with guidelines set out by the gem trade of the West and that after finishing his activities he will guarantee to turn the land back to its original condition, this will take us a very long time to achieve. Although there are movements and committees in our industry that are trying to formalise all mining and to have a globalised certification scheme, they are in grave danger of harming those that they are trying to protect. Trying to enforce such schemes in most of the remote rural gem mining areas in the world, communities that are one hundred to two hundred years behind us in terms of modernisation, will just lead to corruption upon corruption and eventually mean that only big companies will be able to conduct business.

The best way we can help the small prospectors and artisanal miners, is by travelling to these remote locations and to help fund and promote education. We should pass on advanced mining techniques in order to improve their working safety; we should educate about sanitation and health; we should do everything we can to genuinely enhance the lives of those that uncover Nature's treasures for us. This is what I call "on the ground help".

Don't get me wrong, I am not saying there is no place for big mining gem companies and that all mining should be left to artisanal miners. Big companies can often bring stability to areas: they can provide education and often safer working conditions. They help to stabilise the flow of gemstones into the market making it easier for big retailers to promote the gem, however what I am trying to ensure is that we must not squeeze out the little man under the false pretence that we are trying in some way to help.

Gemstones are after all the most precious, luxury item you can own. Whilst romance, love, sunsets and sunrises are free, nothing that you can purchase has so much history, is surrounded by so much folklore and legends than a gemstone. No other luxury goods, requires the commitment and dedication as is provided by the true gemstone adventurer: no other luxury goods connect indigenous people in such inhospitable places to the modern world.

Gemstones - the ultimate luxury item.

It's such a pleasure to read an encyclopaedia that is intermingled with features and written documentaries of visits to mines. Steve has managed to write an encyclopaedia, well the first half anyway, that is full of useful information and is surprisingly unbiased when you realise it is written by someone who is the owner of one of the largest coloured gemstone retailers in the world.

What I find most intriguing is that he genuinely wrote it himself. In today's busy world you rarely get business owners who write their own story, normally they would use a ghost writer and employ several researchers and a typist. However, Steve is a little different and on a recent trip to Brazil I watched as he typed thousands of words as we travelled from one gem mine to another.

"The Lure of Gems" is a fully-loaded encyclopaedia and one of the most comprehensive books I have read (well, this first half). It is written in plain English and I am sure that amateurs and gem experts alike will enjoy both the technical side and the various diaries and photographs of mine visits.

Glenn Lehrer

Photograph.
The Bahia, a beautifully sculpted
5 foot, 450 pound Quartz crystal
with golden rutile needles and is on
permanent display in the lobby of the
GIA in California. Glenn Lehrer created
Bahia in collaboration with Lawrence
Stoller, and has been on exhibition at
the Carnegie Museum in Pittsburgh,
PA. and the Los Angeles Museum of
Natural History.

CONTENTS

CONTENTS

CONTENTS

CONTENTS

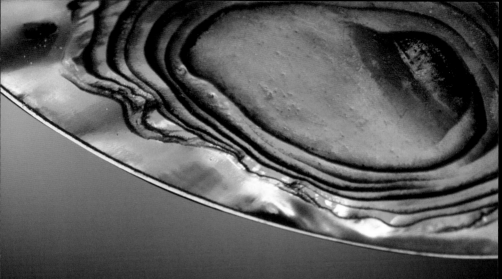

Considered a delicacy by many throughout the world, the Abalone, or Ear Shell, is a Gastropod: a member of the Mollusc family of sea creatures. The creature has a univalve shell, similar to the Limpet and attaches itself to rocks or structures under the sea by suction.

The shell of the Abalone is used in jewellery, and the exceptional and mesmerising colours of the shell are a by-product from farming the shellfish for its meat, making the crafting of jewellery from the Gastropod very eco-friendly.

From one side the shell looks rather dull and unexciting and is quite often covered by other sea crustaceans; but from the other side it shines with an array of stunning colours and beautiful iridescence, displaying

vivid blues, greens and pinks, all combined in a spectacular modern art styled pattern.

Each shell embodies a unique display of colour and markings, almost like the human fingerprint, therefore no two pieces are exactly the same. The gem is ideal for use in many large jewellery designs, from pendants and big, dangly earrings, to bracelets and Sterling Silver rings. In addition to jewellery, you may have seen this gem inlayed into acoustic guitars.

Abalone
A gemstone created in the sea, with a fusion of blues and greens. Just like the ocean's waves with swirling and rolling in beautiful patterns.

In New Zealand the Maori name for the Abalone Shell is the Paua Shell (pronounced Par-war). Therefore when you see the name 'Paua', this refers to Abalone Shell that is only from New Zealand. The best comparison would be Zultanite and Diaspore: Zultanite is Diaspore, but only when it is found in Turkey.

Around its coast line there are both commercial organisations and hobbyists extracting the gem from the sea bed.

Once on dry land, each shell is hand cut, buffed and polished by experts who understand the natural curves and patterns of the shell, ensuring each piece takes full advantage of all the colours of the ocean. I am not sure whether it is due to the shell's array of wonderful colours, or the fact that their next door neighbours often boast about their prized Opals, that many in New Zealand refer to the Paua as 'the opal of the sea'. Without doubt the Paua ranks amongst the finest Abalone on the planet, displaying the most intense blues and greens – which many locals see as mirroring their homeland. As you would expect there are lots of Maori legend and folklore surrounding their local treasure.

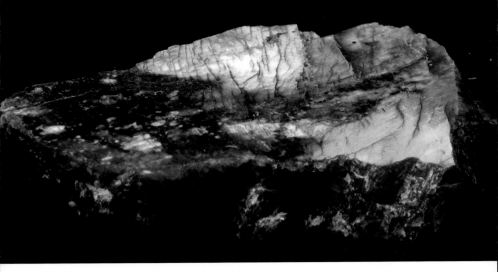

When a gem displays an attractive light, which appears to float below its surface, the effect is known as adularescence. Caused by the physical crystal structure in certain gemstones, it can be seen near the surface of several gems where a ghost-like reflection with a bluish-whitish colour is visible. To maximise this glorious visual effect, these gems are often cabochon cut.

This shimmering effect is visible only in certain gemstones that have a layered type structure. These layers alternate in thickness; the thinner ones are so small that the eye cannot detect the visible wavelengths, scattering the light in multiple directions.

When adularescence is witnessed in Labradorite it is often referred to as labradorescence. In Opals it is known as opalescence, but be careful not to confuse this with 'play of colour', which is a different optical phenomena. Although the effect is most noticeable in Moonstones, Labradorite and Opals, you can occasionally see it in Rose Quartz and some Brazilian Agates.

In Southern Brazil we unearthed some very unusual Lavender Quartz and every single piece demonstrated wonderful adularescence.

Adularescence

Adularescence is a vibrant, natural optical effect similar to the shimmering appearance of the moon on a cloudless evening. Its name is derived from "adularia", a mineralogist term for Moonstone.

Moonstone displaying Adularescence.

Miners travelling to work in the Panjshir Valley.

Afghanistan

Positioned at the crossroads of ancient Indian, Persian, European and Asian civilizations, Afghanistan has been at the heart of gem trading routes and expeditions for thousands of years, which have included such eminent figures as Alexander the Great, Marco Polo and the Moguls.

Unfortunately, today Afghanistan is a country known more for its conflicts. But below ground, gemstone mining is still happening and a kaleidoscope of popular gemstones are being unearthed.

Ruby from Murgab; Spinel from the Kuh-i- Lal mine; Turquoise from Eastern Tajikistan, plus Emerald, Red Jasper, Tourmaline, Amazonite, Kyanite and Garnets: all of these combine to make Afghanistan one of the most prolific countries in the world for gemmologists.

It is said that the famous "Black Prince's Ruby" in the Crown Jewels, which is really a Spinel, originated from the Kuh- i-Lal mine in Afghanistan. Writings by Marco Polo suggest that the mine is one of the oldest gem mines in the world still in operation and records trace its existence back to 101AD. This mine yields not only Spinel, but also Rubies and Garnets. As all three can be similar in colour it is understandable that in years gone by the three gems would often be mistaken by gem explorers, who did not have the scientific tools available to us today.

The mine is a maze of over 400 tunnels, and today's miners occasionally come across ancient bones of miners who were

Ruby miners in Badakhshan discussing the day's mining.

trapped in collapsed mine shafts.

If the fact that Spinel mining took place in 101AD impresses you, then how about the fact that Afghans have been mining for Lapis Lazuli for over 6500 years in the Badakhshan province and Panjshir valley! It has been said by many gemmologists

Various gemstones from Badakhshan.

that Afghanistan has both the largest and best supply of this gemstone in the world.

The landscape of the area is stunning, with the skyline being dominated by the impressive Hindu Kush mountain range which rises to over six thousand metres above sea level (19500 feet).

Like most gem mining in Afghanistan, the area is incredibly difficult to access and if you were to follow the mountain to the East you soon arrive at the heart of the Himalayas and travel across Northern Pakistan and India. As I mentioned in the introduction to this book, gem mining often takes place in the most inhospitable areas and the Panjshir valley is a case in point with its long, freezing cold winters followed by dry, boiling hot summers.

Although it is famous for its Lapis Lazuli, more recently there have also been small discoveries of Emeralds, Tourmaline, Kunzite, Ruby, Aquamarine and Yellow Beryl in the valley. In some sense it is not surprising that this area is rich in gemstones, when you consider the huge geological event that was needed to create the Himalayas. The mountain range was formed as the result of the collision of the Indo- Pakistan and Asian crustal plates.

My gem hunting friend Andy, who works

for the GIA and who kindly took these photos for me in Afghanistan, explains that the Emerald Mines are some of the most difficult of all to reach.

Once you pass several thousand metres the slopes become too steep for the donkeys and the mules to ascend, so the last two hours of the hike up to the Emerald Mine must be

Afghanistan
Tourmaline crystal
from Badakhsham.

done on foot. The air is so thin at this extreme altitude that even for the locals progress is very slow.

Although the area is difficult to reach, I have been told that at its peak there are over a thousand artisanal miners searching for their personal fortune in the area, with over 100 of them working at a small deposit known locally as the Buzmal Mine. Despite the harsh conditions, I have heard that some miners brave the conditions to work virtually the entire year round.

Most Emerald mining in Afghanistan today is run by small family businesses in the Panjshir Valley. These tiny mining operations are located some 3,000 to 4,000 metres above sea level and are extremely difficult to reach. Afghan Emeralds are often more transparent and somewhat brighter than those

found in the likes of Colombia and Siberia.

The Jegdalek mines, located only 40 miles to the East of Kabul, produce some fine quality Rubies and Sapphires. Although the distance is not great, my gem hunter in Afghanistan tells me, "the first part of the journey is on a fairly major road, however, due to the

Kabul market.

recent wars there are many land mines and the route is very treacherous. As you get closer to the mines the road turns to a dirt track and eventually you have to drive along a shallow stream bed." The Jegdalek mines are unusual in that the gems are being mined in a geological belt made up primarily of marble. In some places the marble is up to 900 feet deep. Here there are some 400 mines all being operated by artisanal miners, who in the main only use a hammer and a pick axe. Many of them make shelters out of the rocks they excavate and then once inside chip away at the marble to remove their treasure.

To the North of the Jegdalek Ruby and Sapphire mines are the Kunzite mines in the Mawi Valley which is located in the Kolum district. Here some of the finest quality material in the world is

Female lapidarist cutting gems in Ishkashim.

discovered. The Mawi Valley Kunzites are truly gorgeous and emit wonderful phosphorescence. The Kunzite here tends to grow in large pegmatites and in the middle of the summer up to 500 miners arrive trying to uncover this beautiful and valuable pink Spodumene. Even in the extremely harsh winter my Afghan Gem Hunter, Zeeshan Khan, tells me that a dedicated few still somehow manage to continue mining. To arrive at the area where the gemstones are most likely to occur, miners have to remove around 10 to 20 metres of clay. As with other remote mining areas, the tools they have at their disposal are very primitive indeed.

Throughout history, all of these different mining locations, with their treasure trove of different gemstones, are believed to have helped locals trade their findings for weapons, in order to defend themselves. The country has had so many different conflicts: the Greeks invaded in 327BC, Mongols in 1227, the British from 1838 - 1919, the Russians from 1979 to 1988. All of these wars motivated indigenous tribes people to explore for new gem deposits in order to protect their families.

Mayor of Badakhshan village.

Ruby miner in Badakshan.

Agate

This gemstone has been prized since antiquity and is a variety of Chalcedony, which in turn is a member of the Quartz family.

It was given its name by Theophrastus, a Greek philosopher who is believed to have discovered the gem on the banks of the river Achates in the 4th century BC. The gemstone was later mentioned in the Bible as one of the "stones of fire".

Made from silicon dioxide, it has a glassy (vitreous) lustre, and registers 7 in hardness on the Mohs scale. Being such a hard stone, Agate is often used to make brooches and pins. Additionally, as it can also resist acids (unlike a lot of other gemstones) it has been used to make mortars and pestles to press and combine chemicals.

Many Agates originate in cavities of molten rock, where gas bubbles trapped in solidifying lava are replaced with alkali and silica bearing solutions. Formed as a banded round nodule (similar to the rings of a tree trunk) the gem boasts an exquisite assortment of shapes and colours of bands, which may be seen clearly if a lapidarist cuts the sections at a right angle to the layers: this is sometimes referred to as Riband Agate.

Other types of Agate include Onyx (Onyx is almost always a dyed Agate), Sardonyx, Ring Agate (encompassing bands of different colours), Moss Agate (with green banding), Blue Lace Agate, Turritella Agate,

Colour	Many different colours
Family	Quartz
Hardness	6.5 – 7
SG	2.56 – 2.64
RI	1.530 – 1.550
Crystal	Trigonal
Properties	Vitreous to waxy lustre
Treatments	Dye
Cleaning	Ultrasonic: Usually safe but best with warm soapy water
Care	No special care recommended
Composition	SiO_2 (Silicon Dioxide)

Agate comes in a range of vibrant colours, some natural and some enhanced.

Snake Skin Agate, Rainbow Agate and Fire Agate.

Myths and legends suggest that when a person wears Agate, they become more pleasant and agreeable. It is believed to quench thirst, protect against viruses (including fever) and to cure insomnia. Some tribes in Brazil also believe that Agate can even cure the stings of scorpions and bites from poisonous snakes. Cut off from society often without modern medicines Agate is used for a variety of ailments.

Muslims often have the gem set into a ring and wear it on their right hand and have the name of Allah, Ali, or one of the names of the other eleven Imams inscribed on the ring.

The gem can be found all over the world, but the main sources of gem-quality material come from Rio Grande do Sul in Brazil. It can also be found in the United States - in particular the west; Montana and Idaho - Australia, Italy, and also a very small supply from Madagascar.

Alexandrite

is a very valuable and rare Colour Change Chrysoberyl. It is highly regarded by gem experts, enthusiasts and connoisseurs alike.

Colour	Green to red
Family	Chrysoberyl
Hardness	8.5
SG	3.71 - 3.74
RI	1.746 - 1.755
Crystal	Orthorhombic
Properties	Colour change
Treatments	Sometimes heat treated
Care	No special care recommended
Composition	$BeAl_2O_4$

The gem's uniqueness and value is not often apparent at first sight, but finely faceted, one carat pieces or more rank amongst the most expensive gems in the world – far rarer than even fine Diamonds, Rubies, Emeralds and Sapphires.

It is said that Alexandrite was discovered near the Tokovaya River in the Ural Mountains of Russia, on the same day that Alexander II (1818-1881) came of age. Hence the gemstone was named after the 16 year old future Tsar. This was deemed appropriate not just because it was discovered on Russian soil, but also because its extraordinary ability to change colour from red to green echoed the colours of the Russian flag at that time.

The first person to raise its awareness in public, Count Lev Alekseevich Perovskii (1792-1856), believed the stone to be a variety of Emerald, but noting it had a strange mineral content, passed it for a second opinion to the Finnish mineralogist, Nils Gustaf Nordenskiold.

When initially studying the gem, Nordenskiold was also of the opinion that it was a type of Emerald, but as he was confused by its greater hardness he continued to review it. One evening when working by candle light, he was surprised to see the gem was no longer green but had turned a raspberry red. He then declared the gemstone a new form of Chrysoberyl, which would later be given its own distinct name. Today we know that Alexandrite is in fact a colour change variety of Chrysoberyl.

But now for some bad news! It is a misconception that gemstones that are named "colour change" gemstones physically change colour. The reality is that when viewed under different lighting conditions, the gem only appears to change colour. When you buy a "colour change" gemstone, to view the strongest change you need to view the gem under candescent lighting (direct sunlight), which has high proportions of blue and green light, and then immediately view it under incandescent lighting (for example a light bulb), which has a higher balance of red light. Therefore, when you view Alexandrite in daylight the gem appears green, but when the light source is reddish (incandescent), the gem shows hues of purple or red. Effectively you are looking at an optical illusion! Most changes are incredibly subtle, so the saying that Alexandrite looks like Emerald by day and Ruby by night, is a little bit of an exaggeration. That said, Alexandrite is a real treasure: so incredibly rare that few jewellers have

ever even held a piece!

Not only does Alexandrite have the ability to change colour, it is also a pleochroic gemstone; this means different colours can be seen when the gem is viewed from different angles. The gem is also very durable, measuring 8.5 on the Mohs scale, making it ideal for setting into all types of precious jewellery.

It is also one of three birthstones for the month of June (Pearl and Moonstone being the other two). In times of upset Alexandrite is believed to strengthen the wearer's intuition, and thus helps find new ways forward where logic and practical thinking will not provide an answer; it is also known to aid creativity and inspire one's imagination.

Alexandrite mine in Songea, Tanzania.

Although Alexandrite was originally discovered in Russia, other mines of this treasured gem have since been discovered in Brazil and Zimbabwe. More importantly, finds in Sri Lanka and India are providing great interest for those in the gem industry, as they are believed to be part of the same vein running down vertically from the original source in the Ural Mountains. However, many gemmologists still believe a fine example known undisputedly to have come from Russia is a real rarity with enormous value.

The number one criterion in valuing Alexandrite for me is the amount of colour change, combined with its clarity and then its size. I would happily pay more for a half carat piece which demonstrated an obvious colour shift, than a one carat piece where you had to use your vivid imagination to see any difference. Generally speaking cloudy Alexandrites have more chance of a stronger colour change than clear ones, but if you can find one that has a clean crystal structure and a vivid colour change then you are indeed looking at a very rare gem.

Over a period of millions of years and exposure to high temperature and pressure, the compressed resin eventually becomes Amber. Because it floats on salt water, if you take a stroll along the beaches on the East Coast of the UK, there is a small chance that you may discover your own piece of the precious stone washed up on the shore!

Interestingly enough, until the mid 19th century this was how most Amber was found, and back then it was appropriately named 'Seastone'.

Amber's resin traps all kind of materials, and it is these inclusions which make every piece of Amber unique. The range of inclusions varies from frogs to bugs to leaves; it is not unusual to find a completely preserved fly or insect hidden inside the gem. The wealth of tiny insects trapped inside is due to the fact that when the resin leaked from the tree, it was incredibly sticky as its job was to stop insects from boring into the bark. 'Jurassic Park' may have given us an insight into how the world was a long time ago, but for Zoologists and Geologists, Amber is a lot more resourceful and to-date they have identified over one thousand different species of extinct insects purely by studying the gemstone! It really is a most unique gem, providing a visual snapshot of what life was like around 50 million years ago.

Amber

is one of a few gems that is organic and is created from fossilised resin of ancient trees.

Colour	Mainly orange, but occasionally found in green, brown, red, and bluish green
Family	Amber
Hardness	2 – 3
SG	1.05 – 1.10
RI	1.54
Crystal	Amorphous
Properties	Resinous lustre
Treatments	Heat treated to improve colour
Cleaning	Keep away from extreme heat and boiling water
Care	Warm soapy water
Composition	Carbon, hydrogen, oxygen

The gem can be warm to touch and can create static electricity when rubbed. In years gone by its ability to create static was believed by many to be a magical power. In fact the word "electricity" originates from the Greek word for Amber, "electron". Many people believe that Amber brings good luck and aids well being.

The Baltic States of Estonia, Latvia and Lithuania provide much of the Amber set in jewellery today, as well as the popular Caribbean holiday destination, the Dominican Republic. Although predominately a rich orange colour, Amber can also be found in yellow, honey, brown and green (Green Amber is formed when plantation is trapped within the resin).

Although Amber is most commonly found in the Baltics, it has also been discovered in several other locations around the globe. In keeping with other naming conventions for Amber, where Rumanite is named after its origin of Romania, Simetite which is Sicilian in origin; Burmite is the name given to Amber which is found in Burma.

Even though it is popular with local people, Burmite is often cloudy and therefore hides many of its hidden treasures locked within the gem. Therefore it is normally cheaper than those specimens found in Poland and the Baltics. That said, as many people who collect gemstones and jewellery often like to collect these items based on their origin, at Gems TV we source gems from a wide variety of countries.

It is not unusual to find insects wholly preserved in some pieces of Amber!

Although many believe this sensational gem was first discovered in the UK, Amblygonite was in fact initially discovered in the early 1800s in Germany, by Johann Breithaupt, a mineralogist who was credited with the discovery and identification of 47 different minerals!

Amblygonite is without doubt one of the unsung heroes of the gem world.

I have a real soft spot for Amblyonite: its beauty is mesmerising and whenever I show a piece to someone in my office, the gem never fails to both stir emotions and to impress my guests. The gem's appearance often resembles a cross between Aquamarine and Paraiba Tourmaline. Its colour is tranquil when indoors, however when worn outdoors its appearance is as lively and sparkly as the sun dancing on the surface off the Mediterranean Sea on a summer afternoon. Unfortunately even though Amblygonite is a relatively common phosphate mineral, the supply of gem-quality pieces is very erratic and over the years I have only ever seen a few parcels of the gem being sold in the trade. If Amblygonite was not so scarce, I believe it would be one of the most highly regarded gemstones on the planet. For now it remains a specialist gemstone

Colour	Colourless to light yellow, light pink, green or blue
Family	None
Hardness	5.5 - 6
SG	3.02
RI	1.61 - 1.63
Crystal	Triclinic
Properties	Transparent
Treatments	Normally not treated
Cleaning	Don't expose to extreme heat
Care	Warm soapy water
Composition	$LiAlPO_4F$

that aficionados and connoisseurs fight over whenever a piece is made available for sale.

Its name is derived from the Greek words for 'blunt' (amblus) and 'angle' (gouia), probably due to the unusual angles of the gem's cleavage. It is sometimes referred to as the 'Prophet Stone'.

Amblygonite is most often found in white and pastel shades of green, lilac, pink, and yellow, but rarely is of a transparent gem-quality material.

As the gem is rich in the chemical element lithium, it is often discovered in the same location as Tourmaline and Apatite.

The two largest gem-quality finds of Amblygonite have been in California and France. The current collection on sale at Gems TV was discovered in East Brazil where the Lavra mine, situated at Rio Jequitinhonha (half way between Minas Gerais and the coast), is famous for one of the largest Alexandrite finds in the world. On discovering possibly the most gorgeous Amblygonite ever unearthed, the mine owners partied hard for many days, saying that the occasion was as important as the time when Alexandrite was found. However, their initial excitement did not last long, as very little of the gem has yet been recovered.

Unfortunately, Amblygonite is very difficult to find. It is also a complete nightmare to cut! With four different directions of cleavage, even the very best lapidarists find the gem a real challenge to facet! When the clarity of the gem is of a high standard and when it is discovered with delicate tones it is a real treasure. As it is relatively soft, it is best kept as a collectable or mounted in a pendant or earrings. Occasionally it can be set into rings, usually in a bezel setting so as to prevent the gemstone from being damaged.

Amblygonite is said to soothe and relax all who wear the gem. Crystal Healers believe that the gem reduces anxiety and stress, whilst others claim that it assists with creativity and brings dreams to life.

Specimen quality Amblygonite is found in several counties around the world including the UK, France and Germany: however gem-quality material (as far as I know) is currently only being mined in Minas Gerais, Brazil.

Amblygonite bezel set into a modern design.

Prior to the First World War, clothing and jewellery trends in the UK were created on home soil, with only a little influence from European neighbours. However, by the 1940s American culture was very dominant in Europe.

The influence of Hollywood movies and the prominence of film stars set the fashion in jewellery, make-up, hair and clothes. It was widely believed that Hollywood glamour would rub off on you if you had similar clothes and jewellery, so many in Europe wanted look-a-like copies of outfits and jewellery worn by their screen idols.

World War II in Europe halted production of fine jewellery when metals were rationed. Fine precious metal and gem jewellery was simply not available. Quality costume jewellery, which was flourishing in America, became much more acceptable in Europe. Today however, most jewellery fashion trends often start in Europe. Italy, France, Switzerland and the UK seem to have a greater influence on designs around the globe than those starting in the USA. Probably one of the biggest trends to originate in the USA in more recent times is the rebirth of the Celtic twisted cable, as used in David Yurman designs.

American Influences

Firstly let's start by saying that Americans spell the word used to describe items worn for personal adornment differently. What is known as jewellery in England is spelt "jewelry" in the USA.

Citrine is today hugely popular in America

Amethyst

Throughout history, Amethyst has been one of the most popular and mystical of all gemstones.

Colour	Purple or green
Family	Quartz
Hardness	7
SG	2.65
RI	1.532-1.554
Crystal	Trigonal
Properties	Normally good clarity
Treatments	Can fade slightly with prolonged exposure to sun
Cleaning	No special care recommended
Care	Heat treated to improve colour
Composition	SiO_2 (Silicon Dioxide)

Its use in very rudimentary jewellery can be traced back as far as the Neolithic period (approximately 4000BC), and samples of it set into gold rings have been uncovered in burial sites from around 2400BC.

Amethyst is the name given to purple Quartz and some believe that its name derives from the Greek word "Amethustos", "A" meaning "not" and "methustos" meaning "to intoxicate".

In ancient times, wealthy lords who wanted to stay sober were said to have had drinking glasses or goblets made from Amethyst. While pouring wine for their guests they could serve themselves water, as the dark purple hue of the gem would disguise the colour of the drink so it looked like wine, thus allowing the lord appear to be partaking in a tipple! Following the same theme, it was thought in ancient times if you wished to save a drunkard from delirium you could mix crushed Amethyst into a person's drink.

One legend from Greek mythology tells the tale of Dionysus, the god of intoxication, and a young beautiful maiden, named Amethystos, who refused his advances. Dionysus let loose fierce tigers while Amethystos was on her way to pray to the goddess Diana. Before they reached her, Diana turned her into a statue of pure Crystalline Quartz to protect her from the advancing tigers. Humbled by Amethystos' resolution, and horrified at what he had almost done to her, he wept tears of wine. Legend says his tears turned the colourless Quartz purple, thus creating Amethyst.

Amethyst is mentioned in the Old Testament as one of the twelve stones representing the twelve tribes of Israel and was also one of the twelve gemstones adorning the breastplate of the high priest Aaron (Exodus 39). With its association with piety and celibacy, Amethyst has been set into rings and worn by Cardinals, Bishops and Priests of the Catholic Church since the Middle Ages. Over the years, along with its use by the Church, the gem has also been cherished by royalty and several pieces can be found in the British Crown Jewels. Amethyst was also known as a personal favourite of Catherine the Great.

A bracelet worn by Queen Charlotte of England in the early 1700s was valued at £200 at that time. With inflation that would make it more expensive than the 2007 Diamond Skull created by Damien Hirst! However, shortly after this period a new discovery of Amethyst deposits was made in Brazil, which dramatically reduced the value of the Queen's bracelet.

This provides a good example of how the value of genuine gemstones (just like the stock market) can go up and down based on supply and demand.

When mines are eventually exhausted prices tend to increase; as new deposits are found, gemstone prices generally decrease.

Amethyst occurs in many shades, from a light, slightly lavender pinkish to a deep purple similar to that of the Cabernet Sauvignon grape. Amethyst is also pleochroic, which means that when light hits the gem, shades of different colours such as reds and blues can be seen from different angles.

As there is no single dominant organisation or ruling body relating to gemstones, there are often different approaches to how a gem is graded or named. Many organisations within the jewellery industry for instance refer to Green Quartz as Green Amethyst, while others refer to Green Quartz as Prasiolite, Amegreen or Vermarine! This is a really hot topic in the gem world: some believing that the name Amethyst can only be applied to purple Quartz, others saying if a Quartz's green colour is derived from heat treated Amethyst then it should be named Green Amethyst and others saying it should be known as Green Quartz or Prasiolite.

Most Green Amethyst has been available since the mid 1950s, has come from Brazil and is heat treated and irradiated to produce an electrifying transparent olive-coloured green gemstone. That said, Green Amethyst (or whatever you want to call it!), has been known to appear naturally in a small mine in

Silesia, Poland, and claims of natural Green Amethyst discoveries have also been made in Namibia, Nevada USA, Zambia and Tanzania.

Different tones of Amethyst have different prefixes: "Siberian Amethyst" refers to darker Amethyst regardless of whether they are from Siberia or not, normally having a tone of 75-80%; and Amethyst with a more pinkish tone (20-30%) is named "Rose De France". Amethyst is a hard and durable gemstone measuring 7 on the Mohs scale. In its rough state, the gem often forms in long prismatic crystals, making it ideal for cutting. Because its colour can often appear banded, it is usually cut into round brilliant shapes which helps the gem display a more uniformed colour when viewed through the table or crown facets.

Amethyst is considered a symbol of peace of mind, modesty and piety. Some believe that Amethyst holds powers to change anger to tranquillity and is used by crystal healers to revert negative energy into positive energy. It is popular for its healing and meditative powers, and purifies the mind, body and spirit, helping to realign the chakras. It is also considered an ideal gemstone for those struggling or recovering from alcoholism as it protects against drunkenness.

Amethyst is the birthstone of February. It is also associated with the zodiac signs of Pisces, Aries, Aquarius and Sagittarius. The gem is mined in several countries including the USA, Brazil, Madagascar and Kenya. One of the largest Amethyst mines in the world is in Maissau in Austria and is unusual in that it is open to the public. If you want to travel further, then the Amethyst mines in Brazil are considered to be the best in the world and as long as you don't mind roughing it a little, you're sure to have a great adventure visiting the local artisan miners.

Stunning colours of Amethyst are already present in crystform in this Geode.

A charming Brazilian Amethyst Ring from the Tomas Rae collection.

Amethyst Feature
Alto Uruguai Amethyst

Miners entering the Uruguai mine.

In 2011 I travelled to southern Brazil to visit the small Amethyst mines at Alto Uruguia to learn more about the origin of some of the world's most glorious Amethyst.

In the southern region of Brazil, only 200 miles north of the Uruguayan border lies one of the finest discoveries of Amethyst on the planet in the state of Rio Grande. Alto Uruguai is a hilly

two states of Santa Catarina and Rio Grande do Sul and then forms part of the border with Uruguay and Argentina.

The warm, temperate climate is good for arable farming, with the main crops being soya, maize and beans. What of course interests us the most is what happens under the soil in Alto Uruguia: the discovery of gorgeous

district in Rio Grande do Sul (the southernmost state of Brazil) the area is very rural and sparsely populated, with most people living in isolated farmhouses on small farms. The mining area's name is taken from the great river "Rio Uruguai" which travels through Southern Brazil dividing the

Amethyst with vivid colour and great clarity. The area is not just famed for its purple Amethyst, but also Amethyst that when irradiated turns a stunning green colour (also known as Prasiolite) and breathtaking Lavender Quartz.

Alto Uruguia Amethyst was formed just

before the Jurassic Period when large masses of volcanic lava were flowing from low lying volcanic activity in Southern Brazil. Often trees would get swept along with the lava and over many years these would rot inside the solidified lava and form large pockets (known in geology as vugs). Other pockets were formed in the lava by gas bubbles. Then over a period of thousands of years a hydrothermal process (the movement of hot water) mixed with a cocktail of elements such as iron stopped to rest in these large pockets and formed geodes. Whilst at first glance you would easily overlook their dull grey outer, once cracked open some geodes have a beautiful coloured interior. When did this geological wonder occur? Well, it was during the Cretaceous Period (hence the word cretaceous rock) which started in the Jurassic Period 144 million years ago and is believed to have ended approximately 65 million later.

All of the mines in the region are underground and are mined by small teams, using a combination of explosives, pneumatic drills, hammers

and chisels. Many of the tunnels are around two metres high, just enough height to get small carts and basic trucks inside to extract the ore. We all know the jeep stands for "just enough essential parts", well the truck in the picture on the previous page which miners use to get to the rock face takes the meaning to different level! Mining in the area is a very slow process, as the rock in which the geodes are found is incredibly strong. Depending on its size, once a geode has been discovered the actual extraction process can take several days.

Ametrine is possibly one of the most interesting and beautiful gemstones to become available on the global gem market during recent years.

Ametrine

Discovered only at the Anahi Mine in Bolivia comes a gemstone with a beautiful split personality.

Currently only found at the Anahi Mine in Eastern Bolivia, it is a fusion of the gorgeous regal purple of Amethyst and the warm sunshine hue of Citrine, beautifully combined in one stone. In the gem industry, Ametrine also goes by the name of Bolivianite, due the location of its source.

Ametrine's bi-coloured effect is uniquely created due to differing temperatures across the gem during its crystal formation. The area with the highest temperature forms golden Citrine yellows and the cooler zone forms lilac Amethyst colours. However, this one-off occurrence was a tough trick for Mother Nature to perform, because if too much heat had been applied the entire gem would have become a Citrine.

Many gemstone dealers have tried to emulate this balancing act by heating one end of an Amethyst. However they are all said to have failed as the heat travels too fast through the gem, making it all turn to Citrine. Cutting the rough of Ametrine is such an important task because it can make or break the beauty of the

Colour	Purple to yellow
Family	Quartz
Hardness	7
SG	2.65
RI	1.54-1.55
Crystal	Trigonal
Properties	Bi-coloured gemstone
Treatments	Heat treated to improve colour
Cleaning	Can in rare cases fade with prolonged exposure to sun
Care	Ultrasonic or warm soapy water.
Composition	SiO_2 (Silicon Dioxide)

gem. Usually the lapidarist (a person who cuts and facets gemstones) will cut the gem into longer shapes so as to draw the eye's attention to its unique bi-colours. The gem looks gorgeous in baguette, emerald and octagon cuts.

Many crystal healers believe that Ametrine holds the same metaphysical properties as both Amethyst and Citrine. It will help guide you through meditation, relieves the stress and strain of everyday life and helps to remove negative emotions and prejudices.

During the last 30 years, the gem trade has favoured Ametrine where the split has been 50/50. Only when there was an equal proportion of Amethyst to Citrine were the prices inflated. Today, in a world where individualism is more prevalent than conformism (we no longer all wear the same branded jumper with the big logo on the front as we did in the '80s) the old rules of the 50/50 split have disappeared. Now, we consider the vividness of the colour, the clarity of the Ametrine, the cut of the gem more importantly than the percentage of each colour.

More recently, lapidarists have been cutting Ametrine and deliberately selecting areas where the chocolate wrapper purple of the Amethyst portion swirls, wraps and carelessly merges with the sunflower yellows of the Citrine portion. In Hong Kong where a lot of Ametrine is cut and faceted, they have even invented a new name for this style: "Sunburst Ametrine".

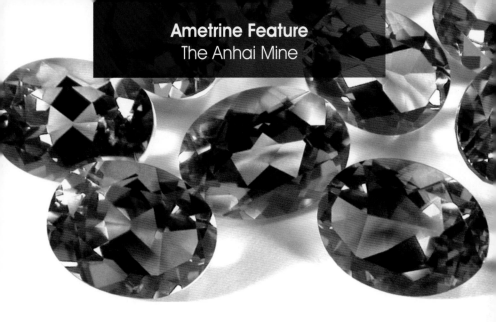

Ametrine Feature
The Anhai Mine

The Anahi Mine is located in Santa Cruz, which is just 20 miles from Bolivia's border with Brazil. The Anahi Mine is the only significant source of natural Ametrine on the planet. The mine is owned by Mr Ramiro Rivero and although we have not yet met personally, Ram is a very good friend of my buddy Rob Weldon, who was born in Bolivia and who works at the GIA as their professional photographer.

Rob and I spent a few days together recently on a mining trip in Southern Brazil and during the trip Rob explained to me all about the operation at Anahi...

Ram's plot of land covers some 6200 acres and is located very near to some of the most beautiful rainforests in the world. Historically the land belonged to the Ayoreo (pronounced "ai-o-reo") who were nomadic hunter-gatherers. All of the mining is now done underground in a network of tunnels similar to the Cruzerio Mine in Minas Gerais. The mine's geologists and mining engineers use all of the latest technology in order to extract their valuable treasure and have a well-educated and highly-skilled team of approximately 70 people. As the location is so remote, they recently built a small grass landing strip next to the mine, making it easier for the mine owners to frequently get in and out of the mine. Prior to this they had to travel for eight hours up the Paraguay River by boat, and then make a three hour truck ride through dense jungle forests.

In addition to its world-famous natural Ametrine, the Anahi mine also unearths small amounts of Amethyst, Citrine and Anahite (also known as Lavender Quartz). The mine is operated with great care to the environment and the owners are said to be working towards a carbon neutral status.

Ammolite is claimed by many to be the rarest gemstone on the planet. Whilst this might be taking it a little far, it is certainly incredibly rare and to-date has only ever been discovered in the isolated region of Southern Alberta, Canada.

Ammolite

A kaleidoscope of iridescent colours displayed on the outside of a fossil and from just one small location on the planet - now that's rare!

If you were to ask me to categorise its rarity, I would put it on a par with Zultanite and Paraiba Tourmaline. The problem with Ammolite doesn't stop with its rarity and just like Zultanite, taking the rough material and converting it into a piece that can be set into jewellery is a real lapidarist's challenge.

Whilst with Zultanite the difficulty is due to its crystal structure having perfect cleavage, Ammolite is very delicate and only forms in wafer thin microscopic layers. Whilst we are talking about the similarities with Zultanite, there is one more! Both gemstones are two of the last gemstones to be credited with an official gemstone status. But before we go into this in more detail, let me explain exactly how this incredibly iridescent gemstone was formed.

You may remember studying Ammonites at school; these are one of the most instantly recognised forms of

Colour	Multi-coloured
Family	Organic
Hardness	Variable
SG	Approx 2.7
RI	1.52 - 1.68
Crystal	N/a
Properties	Very iridescent
Treatments	Set as a triplet
Cleaning	Best with warm soapy water

fossils to be found on the planet. Ammonites looked something similar to a squid and their habitat was warm tropical waters. Along with dinosaurs, they became extinct around 65 million years ago at the end of the Mesozoic Era. The gemstone Ammolite is found on the upper shell of the Ammonite fossil, but only on those found in Southern Alberta. This sort of explains its rarity: here is a gemstone that can only be found attached to a fossil and only on a particular type of fossil that came to rest in just one location. According to local miners, even once they find an Ammonite in the region, only 5% demonstrate any iridescence and of these, only a tiny percentage are of gem quality!

The gem is found near the extremely remote town of Magrath, in an area located near the Red Deer River and the St Mary's River in southern Alberta (the nearest major city is Lethbridge). According to folklore the gem was first discovered by a lady who was part of a Blackfoot Indian Tribe. During a very harsh winter, all of the buffalo disappeared and whilst searching for firewood in deep snow, she came across the gemstone under a cottonwood tree. As she held the gem a spirit contacted her and told her it would act as a powerful talisman and would bring the buffalo back to the tribe.

Back in the Mesozoic Era there was a warm tropical sea area known today as the Western Interior Seaway. Due to the movement of tectonic plates this no longer exists and the area is now some 500 miles from the Canadian coastline. As the sea receded and turned to land the Ammonites became buried in a layer of sediment containing the mineral Bentonite. It was the presence of this mineral in this one location that preserved the wonderful iridescence of the shell and which prevented it from becoming a normal calcite fossil.

Sure enough, the very next day, buffalos were seen near the tribe's camp. Even today, members of the Blackfoot Tribe wrap the gemstone in buffalo hide and use the gem in ritual ceremonies before they go hunting.

So it's incredibly rare, has a great history, but what's it physically like? Well, I mentioned at the very beginning that the layer of Ammolite is incredibly thin. It is also very soft measuring just 4.5 to 5.5 on the Mohs scale. It's also very brittle and very flaky, and will also bleach if exposed to sunlight for long periods. Not the sort of information you want to hear if you're a miner and have just uncovered a piece in the earth! Here is a gemstone that has the appearance of the Northern Lights crossed with a Boulder Opal, it has beautiful patterns like spiders webs and is visually one of the prettiest natural items on the planet, but it's not going to last. Luckily this is the age of modern technology, where we have the ability to preserve real treasures. By delicately removing the thin layer from the Ammonite and re-bonding it to a pre-cut slice of the original fossil and then by topping the gem in transparent natural Quartz, the gem becomes preserved. The Quartz on the top of this triplet is sometimes cut with either parallel bars or checkerboard facets. The interaction of the surface lustre of these facets with the colour play of the gemstone beneath can result in some of the most mesmerising optical effects that you will ever see in a gemstone.

Because the gemstone is normally sold as a triplet, it is not sold by carat weight as this would be very misleading, instead it is valued by its size and its play of colour. The more vibrant the colours and the more kaleidoscopic it is, the more expensive it becomes. Just like Tanzanite and Diamonds have a fairly recognised grading system, so do Ammolites. The very finest Ammolite is graded AA and there are three other grades of A+, A and A-.

Some Ammolites will show just one colour and these tend to be graded either A or A-. For every different colour you see in an Ammolite, you are actually seeing into the gemstone and looking at different layers. Colour derived by iridescence as is the case with Ammolite, is different to the colour of most gemstones where the colour seen is the result of absorption of light. With Ammolite each colour is actually being returned to the eye by the reflection of different layers. The more layers there are, the more colours you will see. When you see reds and greens you are looking at light bouncing back from thicker layers in the structure, whilst the thinner layers deliver mainly blues and violets. Because these layers are never clearly defined, every single Ammolite will look different, each one with its own multi-coloured fingerprint of nature.

Just like Tanzanite, Zultanite and Larimar, Ammolite is only found in one location on the planet. Similar to claims by the biggest mining organizations in all of these single location discoveries, is that Ammolite will run out in the near future. The biggest mining company Korite International go as far as to claim that Ammolite will run out in 20 years time: now that sounds kind of familiar!

DID YOU KNOW?

Gemstones such as Amber, Pearl, Coral, Opals and any others that do not have a crystal structure are referred to as amorphous.

AMORPHOUS

Tom is not your normal gem adventurer. He is a quietly spoken, gentle and very sweet, yet professional type of guy. That's not to say all gem prospectors are loud and aggressive, but in the main the type of people who decide to pump a load of cash into the ground in a vain hope they will hit a vein of gems (sorry for the pun) tend to be just slightly nuts!

I have probably just offended lots of my mining friends who will read this book, but they know it's true: gem prospectors are gamblers, they live on the edge and always believe tomorrow will be the day they unearth the big gem.

Tom is a great guy; very calm and very calculating. He first started his Ammolite business with a bunch of friends who loved abseiling. One day as they descended down a hill top in Alberta, Canada, one of them noticed as the sun shone over his shoulder a kaleidoscope of colour nestled between two pieces of rock. He halted his descent, pulled out his pen knife

and was amazed at the multi-coloured stone that he had extracted.

A few days later he showed it to Tom. Instantly Tom knew what it was as he was familiar with the gemstone mining of Ammolite in the region. Over the following months Tom sent his friends back to the rock face and every now and then they managed to unearth several gorgeous pieces. Tom then set about learning how to turn this incredible multi-coloured, ancient fossil into a valuable gemstone. He hired several lapidarists who had experience of working with this fossilised gem and set about launching his own collection.

In 2010 I met up with Tom and we agreed to represent him in the UK. This, from my point of view, was pretty much a no-brainer decision for me, because over the years I had seen people selling Ammolite in the UK, also mined in this same area for incredibly high prices. I knew as I was dealing direct with the miner I would be able to bring Ammolite to my customers at the lowest prices the world had ever seen.

Earlier this year Tom managed to obtain an official mining licence from the local government to mine an area which is half a mile square. Tom laughs as he tells me that the largest Ammolite mining company has to cross his plot in order to reach their mine. Tom then explained how the licences work. Every single fossil they unearth, they have to send a photo to the local museum, with written details on the piece. The government basically have first refusal on any fossil that they feel is of historical or scientific value. Tom explains that they tend to be very reasonable and that he gets to keep nearly all of the pieces he uncovers.

The land he rents is actually allocated to the Hutterite colony. One of the beliefs of this very religious group is that they should not have their photographs taken. Tom explained that they just recently lost a court case where they had refused to even have their photos taken for their driving licences. Tom said that they were really kind-hearted people and that they would frequently drop by his mine and give him a bottle of their homemade rhubarb wine.

Since the successful launch of Ammolite on Gems TV, Tom has been able to afford a huge 90 ton Catapillar digger and has just started excavation. As of yet, very little has been found, but as all mine owners often do, he tells me that his pay dirt is just around the corner.

His licence is very strict and Tom has to ensure that when he finishes his expedition, whether he finds Ammolite or not, he has to invest in turning the land back to its previous condition. This of course is a huge gamble, as even though there has been Ammolite discovered in the region, there is no concrete proof that Tom will discover it on the strip of land that he has leased.

In the meantime his two good friends continue to abseil down the hillside to ensure that he has enough pieces to supply me every now and then.

Andalusite

This Spanish treasure is undeniably one of the most highly pleochoric gems created by nature.

Andalusite is a transparent to translucent gem that derives its name from Andalusia in Spain where it was first discovered.

The gem is actually a polymorph of two gem varieties: Sillimanite and the hugely popular Kyanite. This means they are identical in chemical composition but differ in crystal structure.

Andalusite is often mistaken for Smokey Quartz, Chrysoberyl or Tourmaline. The gemstone benefits from a very distinct and attractive pleochroism, which lapidarists try to highlight when faceting the gem. Usually, when cutting strongly pleochroic gemstones (Iolite, Tanzanite, Kunzite, etc.), lapidarists typically try to minimize the pleochroism

and maximize the single most attractive colour. Interestingly, Andalusite is the opposite, as all the colours visible in different directions are attractive. Cutters therefore try to orient the gem to get a pleasing mix of its orange, brown, yellow, green and golden colours. When cut successfully, Andalusite looks unlike any other gemstone, displaying patterns of colour dancing around its facets

Andalusite registers 7.5 on the Mohs scale, and in addition to Spain has been discovered in Switzerland, Sri Lanka, Kenya, Mozambique and the USA.

Colour	Brown, green or yellow
Family	Andalusite
Hardness	7.5
SG	3.17
RI	1.63 - 1.64
Crystal	Orthorhombic
Properties	Very pleochroic
Treatments	Heat treated
Cleaning	None
Care	Ultrasonic or warm soapy water.
Composition	Al_2SiO_5

What an interesting world we live in! I have always explained to my jewellery team that you should never state anything about gemstones as an absolute fact and instead should use phrases such as 'currently one of the rarest gemstones on the planet' or 'sources inform us that the gem will no longer be mined within the next 10 years'.

Andesine

Sometimes heated and treated, but always a gem that captures the imagination of all true collectors and connoisseurs.

Remember they used to say Garnet comes in every single colour apart from blue, but then what did they discover in Madagsascar in 1998? You guessed it!

It's so easy to get carried away in an industry where people state things as fact, but in reality this industry should by now, after trading coloured gemstones for over 5,000 years, have begun to realise that Mother Nature is never predictable and

often seems to do things that make even the world's best gem experts occasionally look a little silly.

In 2002 at the world famous Tucson Gem Show in Arizona, when a stunning new gemstone called Andesine exploded on to the scene (well, it wasn't brand new, but we will come to that in a moment), there were many stories and myths surrounding its original location and what in fact

Colour	Red, green or yellow
Family	Feldspar
Hardness	6 - 6.5
SG	2.68
RI	1.54 - 1.56
Crystal	Triclinic
Properties	Possible colour change
Treatments	Heat treated and diffused
Composition	(Ca,Na) (Al,Si)

the gemstone was.

The gemstone is so stunning that the miners of this new source kept its location a real secret and many in the industry incorrectly said that it came from either India or the Democratic Republic of Congo. With so much demand for top quality Andesine, many in the industry were selling very similar pieces and claiming it was from the same source as the very finest material, and as nobody knew exactly where the new source was, nobody could dispute the dealers' claims of origin. Whilst many were uncertain of the location of this new magnificent gemstone, it was certainly being mined somewhere in the Himalayas, a far cry from where it was originally discovered in the 1840s in the Andes Mountains in Bolivia, from where its name is derived.

But what is this gemstone and what is its real name?! Unfortunately, this is still a matter for debate. Firstly a fact: the gemstone is a top quality red gemstone and is a member of the Feldspar family. The finest examples are right up there with Paraiba Tourmaline and Alexandrite. In fact, Andesine shares similarities with both in that there is also a green colour change version of the gemstone which appears very similar to Alexandrite and like Paraiba, part of its magical brilliance is due to the presence of Copper.

At the 2008 Olympic Games held in Beijing, there was a large display featuring many pieces of Red Andesine which had been chosen as the official gemstone of the games. This raised alarm bells in the industry, as it was believed that very little of the gem had ever been discovered in China and Tibet.

On the 31st of January 2011 at the Gemstone Industry Laboratory Conference (the GILC is the most important meeting in the gem trade calendar relating to the technical aspects of our industry), the forty or so delegates spent two hours discussing a recent trip to the Andesine mines of Tibet by several respected members of the trade. Here, we were informed that the group had travelled to the highlands of the Himalayas in Southern Tibet to the Bainang County, which is located some 45 miles south of Tibet's second largest city, Xigaze. The road from the city is nothing more than a dirt track and the group had to ascend to 4000 metres above sea level. In the winter the track is impossible to travel as it is deep under snow and even when the team arrived during the summer they said the air was frigid and very thin due to the altitude.

At the remote area where the mines are located, several families have now set up home. During the time spent in the area, the team did indeed uncover some pieces of natural Red Andesine themselves, but only saw around 10 gem miners in the whole region. The fact that there were so few miners in this remote location led the team to believe that although they had proven that Red Andesine can be found naturally in Tibet, it could not be the only source of the gem.

So where is the majority of Red Andesine being unearthed? The answer lies in Inner Mongolia. This is a country that is landlocked: to its north is Russia and to the east, south and west is China. In terms of geographical size, the country is the 19th largest country in the world spanning a huge 604,000 square miles, yet its population is only 2.9 million. That's the equivalent of the population of Birmingham being spread across a country six times bigger than Great Britain. To the north of the city of Baotou is the small county of Guyang: here in the small villages of Shuiquan and Haibouzi for many years local miners have been excavating small quantities of fine yellow Andesine (some call it Yellow Labradorite as both are plagioclase Feldspars). Since 2003, the main mine just outside of the village has been run by Wang Gou Ping. At the end of each year's harvest, Wang hires 40 or so farmers to mine for the treasured Yellow Andesine. Many of these golden glowing gems are then treated with diffusion and then turn orangeish red, looking very similar to those coming out of Tibet. What are the main differences between Andesine coming from these very different locations, other than one is colour enhanced? As they say in the wine trade, the 'terroir' is very different, a term which expresses the particular characteristic bestowed by the geographical, geological and climate conditions. In Tibet the gems are mined at 4000 metres above sea level, whereas in Mongolia the landscape is very flat. In terms of chemical composition, the gems from Tibet have a lower Ba/Li ratio than those discovered in Mongolia, but have a natural presence of copper.

The conclusion reached from the dedicated work of the team that went to both Tibet and Mongolia in 2010, is that their natural Red Andesine is being mined in Tibet, but the quantities are extremely small. The vast majority of Red Andesine on the market we now believe to have come from Mongolia and has had its colour transformed from a sunflower yellow to a beautiful orangish red colour through diffusion.

When it comes to Green Andesine and Colour Change Andesine, these are incredibly rare and beautiful gems also. The colour change variety has some of the best colour change we have ever seen in a gemstone, having the ability to go from a stunning bottle green colour under florescent lighting, to a glorious almost Amethyst purple colour under a strong torch light.

I received a letter from a lovely customer who had taken her jewellery to be valued and on return was delighted that it had come back at £5000. She was told that the gem was not a Green Andesine but actually an Alexandrite! However, when I was able to examine the piece, I discovered the piece was in fact Andesine and the jeweller had made a basic mistake. Firstly, the two gems look visually different and their refractive indexes are also miles apart! What I always suggest is that when you purchase a rare gemstone, if you want to have it properly valued, you will need to go to an expert in coloured gemstones!

Demantoid Garnet is the most collectable and well-known member of the Andradite Garnet family.

Andradite Garnet

You will see from the gem table that Andradite has quite a complex chemical composition.

Colour	Yellow, Green, Brown or Black
Family	Andradite
Hardness	6.5 - 7
SG	3.84
RI	1.88
Crystal	Cubic
Properties	Vitreous Luster
Treatments	None
Cleaning	None
Care	Ultrasonic or warm soapy water
Composition	Ca3fe2(SiO4)3

The gem receives its wide variety of colours due to the fact that its complex composition can be a cocktail of manganese, aluminium, titanium or chromium.

There are three main members of the Andradite family of Garnets:

Melanite is the black variety of the gem and is not that often seen in jewellery. Its main ingredient is titanium and it is often discovered near volcanoes and in particular old lava deposits.

Topazolite is normally yellow in colour and receives its name for its similarity in appearance to Imperial Topaz. The gem has been discovered in Italy and the Swiss canton of Valais

(the same location that yields the world's finest Marcasite), however it is incredibly rare and very hard these days to find.

Demantoid, the green member of Andradite, is a gemstone that is regarded by many as one of the most collectable of all.

The gem group was named after the Brazilian mineralogist José Bonifácio de Andrade e Silva, who in the 1830s discovered four new minerals. Andradite can also be found in Italy, Switzerland, Norway, Mexico and America.

A .95ct Topazolite from Switzerland.

Angelite

Is a favourite among Crystal Healers, but not a very well known gemstone.

Colour	White, lilac or blue
Family	Anhydrite
Hardness	3.5
SG	2.87
RI	1.56 - 1.61
Crystal Properties	Orthorhombic Vitrous lustre
Treatments	Not normally treated
Cleaning	Careful not to scratch
Care	Warm soapy water
Composition	CaSO$_4$

Recently I received a very excited phone call from a good friend of mine who was in Peru! 'What are you doing in Peru?' I asked him. I thought he must be on holiday as there is very little gem mining in the country. It turned out that one of his friends had just discovered a small deposit of gemstones and had called him in for his opinion.

What had been discovered was a gemstone known as Angelite which is a delicious lilac, pale blue gem variety of Anhydrite (a gem formed from the compression on Celestite over a period of millions of years), so named for its angelic appearance. Anhydrite can also be found in white, grey, blue, pink and red, but only the lilac-coloured variety is known as 'Angelite'. Despite the common occurrence of Anhyrdite, good quality specimens are extremely rare. It is also a fairly new gemstone, having only been discovered in 1987 in Peru.

On the very rare occasion, you may find a piece that is green and similar in appearance to Malachite.

Its hardness of 3.5 on the Mohs scale coupled with its orthorhombic crystal structure makes it ideal for carving figurines and beaded jewellery. In fact, it is believed that the Ancient Egyptians used the Anhydrite rock to carve animal figurines.

Angelite does have a few drawbacks as a gemstone. First it is a little softer than most gemstones, so you need to be careful if you are wearing different gemstones and metals alongside it.

Secondly it should not be immersed in water for long periods or come into contact with chemicals otherwise it may turn into gypsum (incidentally the second softest mineral on the Mohs scale). In fact its name is derived from the Greek phrase 'an hydros' which means without water, as the gemstone is formed when the mineral Gypsum has formed without water and crystallised. When it comes to cleaning it is best just to use a damp cloth or better still a soft jewellery cloth.

So if it has a few drawbacks why is it so hugely popular? The answer is simple: it is both extremely beautiful and is reported to have many healing benefits.

Some people have reported optical properties including an internal play of light, and some specimens fluorescing under UV light.

Throughout this book you will have noticed that we do not talk about crystal healing too much, preferring to concentrate more on the background and technical aspects of gems. However, with Angelite it's hard to ignore some of these beliefs as they appear quite constant regardless of whom you talk to or whichever book or website you read. Now that might be because everyone is copying each other's research and if that is the case let me apologise for jumping on the bandwagon! Healers use Angelite to unblock energy pathways and to balance the thyroid. It is also highly regarded by crystal healers as assisting with communication with other humans, including those who are no longer with us.

I have also read that Angelite is very useful for weight control and although my wife (who is very slim) has yet to wear the gem, in her previous career as a pop singer her stage name was coincidently Angelle!

The gem is believed to be related to the fifth chakra (throat), which helps with communication. Angelite is said to provide the wearer with a heightened awareness and to help one focus on kindness and brotherhood. It is said to promote compassion and understanding and to alleviate psychological pain.

As well as Peru, Angelite has also been found in Germany and New Mexico.

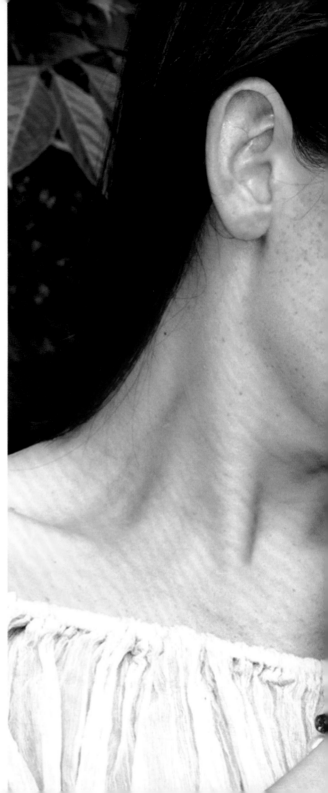

Annabella

Every piece of
Annabella jewellery
is handcrafted to
the finest detail and
features genuine
gemstones set in
beautiful flowing
silver designs.

ANNA BELLA

Did you know that the Pearl is an anniversary gemstone for both the 3rd and 30th anniversary? Citrine celebrates one's 13th anniversary.

Anniversary Gemstones

Anniversaries are traditionally celebrated with the giving of gifts relating to the year of the wedding, civil partnerships or indeed any memorable event.

Around the turn of the 19th century it was popular to give gifts of paper, cotton or leather for the first few years of marriage. However, in more recent times and due to the increasing popularity of fine, rare gemstones, it is more popular to give jewellery to the one you love.

Most people know of the major anniversary gemstones such as Pearl for 30 years, Ruby for 40 and Diamond for 50, but did you know there is in fact a gemstone for every year up to 25 years?

Although there are several variations for a few of the anniversaries, the table on the right details those we believe to be the most universally adopted.

This list of gemstones to celebrate the day that two people made a life time commitment to one another is reported to have been collated by the American National Association of Jewellers in 1912. Since the list was compiled there have been very few discoveries of new gemstones. When you consider how much the world has changed over the past 100 years, its quite comforting to know that one thing remains pretty constant, and that is our love affair with gemstones. However, there has been one major discovery, a discovery that stopped people talking of the big four gemstones and made them increase this to the big five and that is of course Tanzanite. As with the official list of Birthstones which has been modified to include Tanzanite as a December Birthstone, the Anniversary list has added Tanzanite as the 24th Wedding Anniversary gemstone.

For the first 25 years of marriage there is a gemstone or precious metal assigned to each year and thereafter for every fifth year. Notice also how the list still retains precious metals for the 1st, 25th and 50th wedding anniversaries. If you were able to celebrate your 80th anniversary (bearing in mind there have only been a handful of people who have reached this), just think of all the beautiful jewellery you could acquire, and what better reason for it?!

One of the loveliest emails I ever received from a gentleman (stay with me on this one!), was from someone who had found our website while searching on Google to find an anniversary present for his wife. He admitted to have known nothing about gemstones prior to finding our site, but on seeing that Amethyst was the suggested gift for the 6th Wedding Anniversary, he decided to purchase a ring for his wife. His wife was delighted with the gift and commented on how much thought and research he must have put in to find the most appropriate of gifts and on how much he must have spent! He finished his email by saying that the best thing of all, was that the ring cost less than the bunch of flowers he gave her the year before and that he would be back in 12 months' time to buy Onyx!

YEAR	GEMSTONE
1	ANY GEM SET IN GOLD
2	GARNET
3	PEARL
4	BLUE TOPAZ
5	SAPPHIRE
6	AMETHYST
7	ONYX
8	TOURMALINE
9	LAPIS LAZULI
10	DIAMOND
11	TURQUOISE
12	JADE
13	CITRINE
14	OPAL
15	RUBY
16	IMPERIAL TOPAZ AND PERIDOT
17	AMETHYST
18	GARNET
19	AQUAMARINE
20	EMERALD
21	IOLITE
22	SPINEL
23	IMPERIAL TOPAZ
24	TANZANITE
25	ANY GEM SET IN SILVER
30	PEARL
35	CORAL AND EMERALD
40	RUBY
45	ALEXANDRITE AND SAPPHIRE
50	GOLD
55	ALEXANDRITE AND EMERALD
60	DIAMOND
65	SPINEL
70	SAPPHIRE
75	DIAMOND
80	RUBY

Antique Cushion Cut

One of the most romantic gem cuts of all time

Also known as an "Antique Cut" or "Pillow Cut", the antique cushion cut in appearance is similar to the "Old Mine Cut", which was popular in the late 19th century, and the more modern "Oval Cut".

The Antique Cushion Cut is occasionally used for Diamonds. Although the cut does not have the same ability to display dispersion as the brilliant cut, it is however very romantic in appearance as it is reminiscent of cuts applied to Diamonds worn by previous generations. The cut is often applied to coloured gemstones and can dramatically increase the flashes of lustre seen from the crown of the gem.

Often you may hear the cut being referred to as the Candlelight Cut. The reason for this is that in the early 1900s, before the light bulb was in every home, the Antique Cushion Cut was said to bring out the fire (dispersion) in a Diamond better than any other cut.

During the Art Deco period, the cut was extremely popular in Engagement Rings. The Graff Diamond and the Hope Diamond (the most written about coloured Diamond on the planet and said to be cursed) are both a variation on the Antique Cushion Cut.

An antique cut Tanzanite.

Although Apatite is really a family of gemstones, as the individual members have very long and difficult-to-pronounce names, the jewellery industry tends to use Apatite as the generic name.

Apatite
Famous for its swimming pool blues to lively light greens.

Historically, because the gem was often confused with other gemstones such as Tourmaline, Peridot and Beryl, its name is derived from the Greek meaning "to deceive".

The more common colours for Apatite are similar to Paraiba Tourmaline, with swimming pool blues through to lively light greens. That said, other colours occasionally occur: colourless to white, brownish-yellow, greyish-green and one known as the "Asparagus stone" due to its resemblance to the vegetable. There is also a 'Cat's Eye Apatite', which is a rarity at Apatite mines. As you would guess from its name, this type of Apatite displays the optical effect of Chatoyancy, an effect caused by tiny fibrous inclusions that are naturally arranged in a parallel configuration. When the light hits the surface of the polished gemstone, a narrow line of light appears, which looks very similar to the opening and closing of a cat's eye.

Colour	Swimming pool blues through to lively light greens
Family	Apatite
Hardness	5
SG	3.1 – 3.2
RI	1.63 – 1.65
Crystal	Hexagonal
Properties	Strong pleochroism
Treatments	Not normally treated
Cleaning	Be careful not to scratch with metal
Care	Warm soapy water
Composition	$Ca_5(PO_4)_3$ (F,Cl,OH)

Finds of Apatite over 1 carat are very rare indeed, and it is also very difficult to find clean Apatite stones over this size, as many will still have a few inclusions. That said, if the colour saturation is good, then even with inclusions you still have yourself a rare and beautiful piece.

The recent finds of Apatite in Madagascar in 1995 have added to the popularity of this gem. Exhibiting excellent saturation, Madagascan Apatite's colours range from neon "Emerald" greens (as typified by our Fort Dauphin Apatite) to neon "Paraiba" blues.

Even rarer than gem-quality Apatite is the purple variation of this gemstone, found in the Mount Apatite of Maine, USA.

Apatite has been associated with many healing properties and is a gemstone often combined with other

Apatite stones with fantastic clarity and colour saturation are a real find.

Apatite crystals

gems to further its healing powers. It is also thought to be an aid to seeing the truth about oneself.

When you combine Rose Quartz with Apatite it is meant to draw and give

unconditional love; if you pair it with colourless Quartz it can help you see the changes that need to occur in your life; and when combined with Aquamarine it is believed to help you make those changes.

For such a beautiful gemstone, with almost a neon glow, it is difficult to comprehend how many Apatites are created from fossilised dinosaur bones! At just 5 on the Mohs scale, Apatite is one of the softest gems to be set in jewellery, but treated respectably its alluring and luscious glow will keep its owner entranced for many years.

Deposits have been found in several locations including Cornwall in England, Canada, Norway, Russia and Sweden.

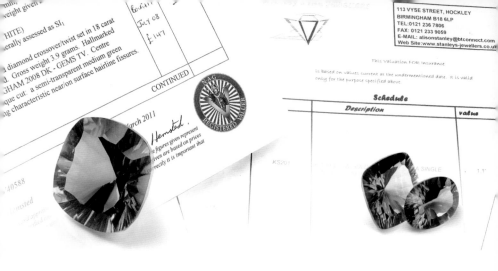

I have put appraisals and valuations under two separate headings. The reason for this is that whilst valuations are often sought by people wanting to insure their items, they are not often of a technical nature. Whilst valuations of gold and diamond jewellery can be done on most high streets, there are very few places - certainly in the UK - where you can get a full appraisal of a coloured gemstone. If you are fortunate enough to have inherited jewellery and it is set with beautiful gemstones, you may want to have it professionally appraised, because you may be surprised with what you have.

Appraisals are a worthwhile investment for your most prized possessions.

A good friend of mine who appraises jewellery once had a customer who wanted her beaded necklace valued because it had a nice Emerald on the clasp. She could hardly believe her luck when she was informed that the beads were all very high grade and incredibly rare Imperial Jade and that the piece was worth over £100,000!

If you have a coloured gemstone and want to find out more about it, be sure to go to a coloured gemstone specialist. Make sure they have not only been trained to the highest level in

RECOMMENDED ORGANISATIONS FOR VALUATIONS OF GEMSTONES	
LABORATORY	**WEB ADDRESS**
Safeguard Part of the Assay Office Birmingham	www.theassayoffice.co.uk/safeguard/
Gübelin Gem Lab Ltd of Switerland	www.gubelingemlab.ch
GI International Gemological Institute Antwerp	www.igiworldwide.com
GIA Gemological Institute of America	www.gia.edu
EGL European Gemological Laboratory Antwerp	www.egl.co.za

coloured stones, but also make sure they are using up-to-date equipment. The reason why I recommend this is that there are so many treatments and enhancements constantly being developed for gemstones, that unless the appraiser has the latest technology, they may make incorrect assumptions.

A little knowledge is also a dangerous thing and my good friend Glenn Lehrer who is one of the most highly skilled gentlemen in the coloured gemstone industry, tells a wonderful story which highlights the above point. "A lady once walked into my store in San Francisco to have some pieces valued, as she was leaving I noticed she was wearing a lovely ring, so I asked her why she did not want it valued along with her other pieces. She said 'oh, unfortunately this piece is just a synthetic Sapphire but I wear it for sentimental reason.' So I asked her if she minded if I took a look. Even without a loupe, I could tell this Sapphire was in fact genuine. So I politely asked her to remove it so I could view it under a microscope. She looked a little confused with my

level of excitement but agreed with my surprising request. Through the lens I could clearly see a pattern of inclusions consistent with either a Burmese or Ceylon Sapphire. I asked her why she thought it was synthetic and she said that she had once had it valued by a dealer in town who told her it was synthetic.

"I asked her to step behind my counter and have a look for herself in the microscope, I asked her if she could see the patterns of lines and once she acknowledged them for herself, I told her that it was actually a very rare and beautiful coloured Sapphire, which I could tell from my observations had not even been heat treated. It was worth a small fortune."

Now as Glenn lives in San Fransisco, you might find it uneconomical to send your pieces to him for appraisal, therefore I have listed above some of the best laboratories in Europe.

I had a similar experience only a few months ago: a customer bought a stunning 4.8 carat Tanzanite from us

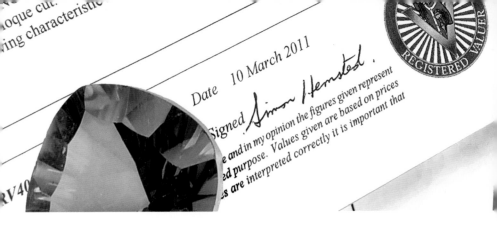

set into 18k gold. She took it to her local jeweller for an evaluation and left the building furious with us as the man in the store said it was not really worth more than £100. However, he liked the design of the piece and was therefore happy to offer her a really good price of £200 for it. The customer left the store in floods of tears and after having a coffee called my office and asked to speak to me directly. After I managed to calm her down I asked her to explain the full story. I looked at her account on our computer and found the full details of what she had purchased. I told her that she was very lucky that she did not sell it. Firstly, I explained to her that even the scrap value of the gold was worth more than £200 to the jeweller! This amazing ring had over half a carat of quality diamonds and the jeweller could probably have sold those in his store for another £800. So already he should have offered her £1000.

Most importantly, the Tanzanite was of a very high grade and without blowing our own trumpet, I find it highly unlikely that there is anyone in the UK that buys as much Tanzanite as we do and could source the gem at a lower price

and I could see that we had paid over £900 for the loose gem. I asked the customer to send the piece to a proper lab and gave her the address of several to choose from. I had originally sold her the piece for less than £2000 and so I made her an offer; I said "If you send it to any of these accredited laboratories, and they do not appraise it for more than my company sold it to you, then I will not only pay for the appraisal, but I will take it back and give you a full refund". Interestingly, the customer never called me back!

But what information can you get if you invest in a professional appraisal? Well, firstly you will be informed about the purity of your precious metal (not all gem laboratories automatically do this so if you want your metal assayed it's best to check with them first). Most importantly though, you want to know more about your gem. You want to know if it is genuine, laboratory grown or synthetic. Once that it is established that your gemstone is of a natural origin, you may also like to find out what enhancements it has had. For some gemstones, quality laboratories will often even tell you the most likely country of origin.

Aquamarine

is one of the world's most popular and well-known gemstones. Often found with great clarity in a light yet energetic blue.

Colour	Light blue
Family	Beryl
Hardness	7.5 – 8
SG	2.68 – 2.79
RI	1.567 – 1.590
Crystal	Hexagonal
Properties	Normally has good clarity
Treatments	Heat treated to enhance colour
Cleaning	No special care needed
Care	Ultrasonic, steam cleaner or warm soapy water
Composition	$Be_3Al_2Si_6O_{18}$ (beryllium, aluminium)

Aquamarine is a real favourite of many gem collectors and in a world that's becoming more and more polluted, Aquamarine offers us all a breath of fresh air.

A member of the Beryl family, Aquamarine's characteristic pale blue colour is created by the presence of iron. Likewise, all members of the Beryl family obtain their colours by the presence of metallic elements, without which pure Beryl remains colourless.

Gemstones that are coloured by nature in this way are known as allochromatic. Aquamarine's younger sister Morganite is coloured by manganese, and its older and more complicated sister, Emerald, receives her personality from the presence of chromium, iron and vanadium.

Its name is derived from the Latin "aqua" for "water" and "mare" for "sea", and many superstitions and legends regarding the sea have been attached to the gemstone over the years. Believed to be the treasure of mermaids, the gem is said to be especially strong when submerged in water. When its powers seemed to dwindle, the gem would be placed in water on the night of a sparkling full moon.

In times gone by, as a very last resort, sailors caught in a storm were believed to throw their Aquamarines overboard to calm the gods. Sailors were also said to have taken Aquamarine to sea as a lucky charm to protect against shipwreck, and many people today still wear Aquamarine to prevent travel sickness.

Back on shore, Aquamarine is believed to both soothe and prolong relationships, and for this reason is often given as an anniversary gift way before its official listing for one's 19th anniversary. For those frightened of spiders or flying, wearing Aquamarine is said to suppress one's phobias.

Out of the ground, many Aquamarines have a slight green tint and are often heat treated to turn the gem into a more pure blue. However, over recent years, the lighter, natural colour has become very popular amongst gemstone collectors. In either shade, this birthstone for March is highly sought after for its clarity, transparency and undeniable calmness.

Similar to Amethyst where different shades are given different prefixes, Aquamarine also has a different prefix relating to its colour. Santa Maria Aquamarine describes those with a deeper shade of blue than normal. The name is derived from the Santa Maria de Itabira gem mines of Brazil, where deep and vibrant Aquamarines have been found - not, as some people believe, from the name of the ship on which Christopher Columbus made his first cross Atlantic voyage,

or indeed from Santa Maria city in California.

The largest source of Aquamarine is found in the state of Minas Gerais in south-east Brazil, but today Africa is becoming a strong rival, with mining activities in countries such as Madagascar, Mozambique, Nigeria and Tanzania.

Aquamarine receives its colour from the presence of two types of iron, ferrous and ferric. Ferrous iron provides the gem with its trademark blue colour, whilst the presence of ferric iron turns the gem slightly green. Normally in its rough state, as when it is mined, Aquamarine is more of a greenish blue. To remove this secondary colour, the rough is normally heat treated before it is sent for cutting, converting ferric iron to ferrous iron. Unusually, as it does not take a high temperature to purify the colour of Aquamarines, it is undetectable in nearly all laboratory tests. For this reason it is always best to assume that any Aquamarine you purchase has been heat treated. As the heat treating does not intensify the tone of the Aquamarine (it only turns its green hues to blue) some gem collectors prefer Aquamarines that feature their natural greenish blue colour.

The darker an Aquamarine, the more desirable and valuable it becomes. Normally its tone ranges from just 10 to 30% tone and once into the high twenties it is often referred to as Santa Maria Aquamarine. Some Aquamarines will appear almost colourless in normal daylight and yet display a beautiful tone under the light of a candle or a light bulb; so much so that it is known as an evening gemstone.

Although today the prefix "Martha Rocha" is often used more to describe some of the finest Kunzites, it was initially used as a descriptive word for Aquamarine. In 1954 a huge glowing Aquamarine was discovered in the Brazilian town of Teofilo Otoni and was named after the winner of the Miss Brazil competition that year, whose eyes were said to have been of the same colour.

A 195 ct Aquamarine on display in the Gems TV museum.

Aragonite is a unique mineral gemstone, as it has the same chemical composition also found in organic molluscs. The crystal structure of Aragonite is also very unusual in that it is often found in needle-like, six-sided prisms.

In addition to its initial discovery in Spain, three large Aragonite caves have also been discovered in Slovakia, Mexico and Argentina.

The cave in Slovakia is buried deep in the Slovak Metalliferous Mountains between Jelsava and Stitnik. Known as the Ochtinska Aragonite Cave, it was discovered in 1954 and was opened to the public in 1972. Unlike most public caves full of stalactites or stalagmites, the unusual crystal structure of Aragonite resembles small shrubs and bushes. One of the main attractions at the mine is the Milky Way Hall, where Aragonites high in the ceiling shine like the stars in the Milky Way. In gemstone terms, the Aragonite in the mine is fairly young; dating back just 13,000 to 100,000 years.

Crystal healers believe that Golden Aragonite is important to the 3rd Chakra and White Aragonite benefits the 7th. I also read Aragonite is suggested as a healer for painful knees.

Aragonite
is named after the Molina de Aragon mine in Guadalajara, Spain where the gem was discovered in 1788 (the mine is situated close to the town of Aragon).

Colour	White, Grey, Yellow or Brown
Family	Aragonite
Hardness	3.5 - 4
SG	2.94
RI	1.53 - 1.68
Crystal	Orthorhombic
Properties	Vitreous Lustre
Treatments	None
Cleaning	Careful not to scratch
Care	Warm soapy water
Composition	$CaCO_3$

From the high Art Deco period, the mid-1920s, comes this exquisite and rare creation. Four French cut Diamonds are arranged in a square forming a one and a half to two carat square Diamond.

Art Deco

It was the age of jazz, prohibition and the Charleston. Queen Victoria was no longer on the throne, but countless ideals and influences from her age still remained.

It was the 1920s, and the world was about to see a profound new style that would change history forever. The style would be known as Art Deco. It was bold, lavish and elegant and was to radically change the art world, leaving a lasting impression that can still be seen today.

After the Universal Exposition of 1900, a group of French artists created a formal collective which was known as 'Société des Artistes Décorateurs' (The Society of the Decorator Artists) of Paris.

Not entirely of their making, the Art Deco 'movement' began more as an amalgamation of numerous different styles and movements of the early 1900s. Art Deco affected architecture, painting, film, both interior and industrial design,

and, most importantly, fashion. Jewellery that came out of the Art Deco movement was forward thinking and extremely bold. Its "in your face" style represented the fast modernization of the world around it.

Art Deco made vast use of triangular, angular and geometric shapes, employing symmetry and repetition. The movement attempted to combine mass production with high-quality art and design. Tiaras, cameos and lavalieres from the

Art Deco Sapphire & Diamond bracelet.
Image courtesy of Lang Antiques
www.langantiques.com

Victorian era were now unpopular, and gave way to fashionable cocktail rings, long pendants and bangle bracelets.

Accessories became popular again: elaborately detailed cigarette cases and ladies compacts were all ornately jewelled and became just as important as earrings, necklaces and bangles. Inexpensive stones such as Coral and crystal were used with platinum and gold. It has been suggested that this opulent and lavish style was a reaction to the hard times and rationing of WW1.

The fundamental difference that made the Art Deco period so extraordinary was that the same design ideas put into jewellery were also being engineered in buildings, ships and even household appliances.

Diamonds began to be cut in new and exciting shapes never seen before. Many of these, such as pear cut, emerald cut and marquise cut were extremely similar to the cuts we see today. These new-found gem cuts blended in with the symmetrical and geometrical nature of the jewellery itself.

Colour played an important role in the Art Deco movement: everything became bold, vibrant and vivid. The way colour was applied was often dramatic; reacting to the light, neutral colours used during the previous Art Nouveau period. Gemstones such as Ruby, Emerald, Sapphire, and Coral became popular for this reason.

Images courtesy of Lang Antiques.

Images courtesy of Lang Antiques www.langantiques.com.

Art Nouveau

(1880 - 1914)
Art Nouveau was
a rich, decorative
and poignant era.
Its objective was
not to imitate,
but to evoke.

Beginning in the later years of Queen Victoria's rule, and carrying on well into the 20th century, the name of the movement 'Art Nouveau' comes from 'Maison de l'Art Nouveau', a shop in Paris that displayed art of this design. The words 'Art Nouveau' are French and simply mean 'New Art'.

Although the movement as a whole lasted about 35 years, the period in which jewellery was created in this style was much shorter lived; only lasting about fifteen years. However, its influence is not to be underestimated as it has gone on to inspire many styles for years after its original popularity decreased.

Art Nouveau was groundbreaking. It marked a time where designers would start looking at the world around them, taking stimuli from the natural world, rather than looking into history for inspiration. The style was a reaction to mass produced jewellery, popular towards the end of the Victorian period. The jewellery was bold, expressive, exotic and exuberant.

When the first few examples of 'Art Nouveau' were showcased in Paris, there was outrage. It represented a radical change, and was different to anything most people had ever seen. Viewers either loved it or despised it. The 'rebellion' was said to have freed a creative energy that had been suppressed for so long.

Art Nouveau incorporated highly stylised designs with flowing, elongated, curving lines. Inspiration came from a wide spectrum, often from nature: ferns, roots, buds, spiders and dragonflies. Snakes became an unlikely popular symbol of life, sexuality and eternity. Unusual designs based on flowers and plants that had not been used before in jewellery were experimented with. Peacocks, and particularly their feathers, became fashionable and were featured in all types of jewellery.

Art Nouveau also used the female form in all its glory, proudly displaying it on necklaces and earrings. The women would have long flowing hair, celebrating the natural woman and her new place in society.

One of the defining techniques of the Art Nouveau period was enamelling. It was used to create patterns or pictures on the desired object, by fusing powdered glass to the surface. The most popular type of enamelling used was known as "Plique a'jour", which gave an effect that has been likened to stained glass. Plique a'jour gave the jewellery a distinct, almost three-dimensional effect, which was unique to the time. It was notoriously hard to do, and was a sign of the artist's skill. Other types of enamelling were 'basse-taille' and 'guilloche.'

An Art Nouveau ring set with a Black Opal and Seed Pearls. The navette ends decorated with black and green enamel.

85

Birmingham Assay Office

Assay

Many countries have laws that govern how precious metals are sold and often, to protect the consumer, insist that a hallmark is applied. Assay is the name of the test that is carried out, before the relevant hallmark is applied.

In the UK, it is a legal requirement for all gold jewellery over 1 gram and all silver jewellery over 7.78 grams to be officially hallmarked by the British Assay Office.

There are four main assay offices in the UK; all of whom have their own hallmark. All items assayed in Birmingham have an anchor stamped into them; Sheffield, a Rose; Edinburgh, a castle; and London, a leopard.

The hallmark includes the purity of the metal: 375 being 9k gold; 585 being 14k gold; 750 being 18k gold; and 925 being Sterling Silver. It is also a legal requirement for the hallmark to carry the sponsor's mark; this is normally the initials of the jewellery importer, retailer or the manufacturer.

In the UK there is also an option for the hallmark to carry a year symbol, which is intended to help further generations trace jewellery back to the date their possession was hallmarked.

In the UK the history of assay testing and hallmarking precious metals dates back to 1300. Under the instruction of Edward I, hallmarking became a legal requirement for Pewter, Silver and Gold in order to protect the public against fraud, and to protect legitimate traders against unfair competition.

This includes a Zircon discovered at Jackson Hills in Western Australia, which has been scientifically dated to have formed 4.4 billion years ago, right near the time the Earth itself was being formed.

In July 1994, the Opal was declared Australia's National Gemstone. Not surprising when you realise that the country supplies more than 90% of the world's gem-quality Opals. Mining for Opals isn't restricted to one area either, but takes place virtually all over the country.

It is believed that Opals were first discovered in Australia in the 1840s by a German gemmologist named Professor Johannes Menge, approximately 50 miles north of the then capital of South Australia,

Adelaide. In the 1870s, while samples of the gem had been sent to the UK for evaluation, the first registered mining leases were being signed in the town of Quilpie (later famous for the 'Pride of the Hills' Opal mine).

Around 1900 Black Opals were discovered by children playing outdoors at Lightning Ridge (thank goodness they didn't have computer games in those days, or we may never have found this fantastic gemstone). Mining in the region at the famous "Shallow Nobby's Mine" started in

In 1994 Opal was declared the national gemstone of Australia

1903 after a miner by the name of Charlie Nettleton walked 400 miles to set up his operation. The mine is still in operation today.

In 1915, teenager Willie Hutchinson discovered an Opal in South Australia, while panning for gold with his father, Jim Hutchison. This crucial find led to the establishment of the world's largest Opal mine named "Coober Pedy" - which, believe it or not, originates from aboriginal dialect meaning "white man in a hole".

Today it's a lot more than just a 'white man in a hole', as the town, with over 3,500 people and 45 different nationalities, is based both above and below ground. In its underground Opal mines one can find: a museum, houses, churches, gift shops and even a hotel. As far as mines go, Coober Pedy really is a rare place!

Today, for the first time in its history, Australia has now got some serious competition for its national treasure, as a recent discovery of opal in Ethiopia has uncovered a quality of gemstone that is very similar in look and appearance and one gem expert has claimed it to be "equal to if not better than Australian Opal" .

Australia is the only country where Mookite is found, in Mooka Creek in Western Australia. Emerald, Agate, Jade, Zircon and Chrysoprase are also discovered in smaller quantities.

Whilst Opal mining always used to be the main gem topic in any Australian bar, today talk of the Argyle Diamond Mine in north-west Australia is rife.

This Diamond mine in the region of Kimberley is said to now be the biggest single producer of Diamonds in the world.

As well as being the world's largest Diamond mine, according to the website owned by the mining company Rio Tintoretto, "the Argyle Diamond Mine produces virtually the entire supply of the world's Pink Diamonds". They also claim to extract approximately 20 million carats of Diamonds per year.

When the mine first opened in 1985, most of the workforce was flown to the mine on a weekly basis from Perth. Over time, as the mine became established, the local towns have become more populated and now most workers have relocated. What is also quite unusual about Argyle is that it is one of the few Diamond deposits that is not hosted in kimberlite.

Australia is also one of the largest blue Sapphire suppliers in the world. Unfortunately as supply of the gem has started to dry up in Burma and Thailand, many cutting houses in Thailand have incorrectly labelled their gems as originating from their own country, in an attempt to play down the rising success of the Australian Sapphire. The gem was first discovered in the Cudgegong River in New South Wales in 1851 when miners stumbled across the gem whilst panning for gold. There are now three main deposits: two in Queensland and one in New South Wales.

Labradorite can sometimes display aventurescence.

This optical effect happens within certain gems which feature a large amount of small disk or plate like inclusions of a mineral with a highly reflective surface (usually haematite, Pyrite or goethite). These inclusions act like tiny mirrors and produce one of nature's most fascinating optical effects.

In the mid-18th century, an Italian glass blower was said to have accidentally knocked a jar of copper filings into the molten glass he was using to create vases, and to his surprise the result was a beautiful glass featuring a metallic sparkle. The technique became widely adopted across Europe where it was used to make both jewellery and ornaments. The glass became known as "ventura", which was derived from the Italian word meaning "by chance". During the following century, a Green Quartz was discovered in Brazil which naturally produced a similar appearance to the Italian glass and was therefore named Aventurine. This is one of the few occasions in gemmology where a gemstone has been named after a manmade item. In addition to Aventurine, only a handful of other gems have been discovered that demonstrate this stunning lively effect, such as Moonstone, Sunstone and Labradorite.

Aventurescence

If a gem's surface appearance looks metallic or as if it is painted with glitter, it is said to display aventurescence.

Aventurine

is a member of the Chalcedony Quartz family and is easily identified by its translucent yet sparkling appearance.

The appearance of Aventurine is so striking that its name is also used as a gemstone adjective when describing other gems with a similar sparkling optical effect: "Aventurescence".

Colour	White, Grey, Yellow, Brown or Green
Family	Chalcedony Quartz
Hardness	3.5 - 4
SG	2.94
RI	1.53 - 1.68
Crystal	Orthorhombic
Properties	Vitreous Lustre
Treatments	None
Cleaning	Careful not to scratch
Care	Warm soapy water
Composition	CaCO$_3$

Aventurine gets its name from the Italian word "per avventura" - which means "by chance". It is believed that in the 18th century, Venetian glass makers accidentally mixed in copper filings while producing their work and the result was a glass that sparkled.

Although green is the predominant colour for this gem, it can also be found in blue, yellow, reddish brown, greenish brown, orange and a most striking pale silvery colour.

Green Aventurine is associated with luck, chance and opportunity and is also believed to increase perception and develop creative insight.

Some highly superstitious people never buy a lottery ticket without their lucky Aventurine in their left pocket (the left pocket is chosen because both luck and left start with "L").

Aventurine is also said to increase your libido and with Tourmaline is the anniversary gemstone for the 8th year of marriage.

Blue Aventurine is said to be a powerful healer that increases positivity and builds inner strength and self discipline. Several people have written that they have felt powerful and assured when wearing Blue Aventurine. If you're a non-believer in myths and legends, Aventurine remains a truly beautiful coloured gem, whose lively sparkling mica flecks will have you spellbound,("mica" is thought to come from the Latin word "mica" meaning "a crumb", most likely derived from "micare", which means "to glitter").

Aventurine has been set in jewellery for many centuries and as it is typically found in larger sizes than many other gems, has also been used to create vases, bowls and even smoking pipes. Aventurine can be found in Brazil, India, China, Japan, the Ural Mountains in Russia, Tanzania, and the USA.

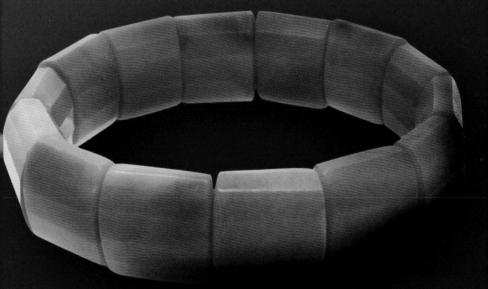

Taking advantage of the larger sizes Aventurine is found in, this Peach Aventurine bracelet offers a natural big look.

Axinite

'Rare', 'stunningly beautiful' and 'a real collector's gemstone', are the first things that pop into my head when I am asked about Axinite.

Colour	Yellow to brown
Family	Axinite
Hardness	6.5 - 7
SG	3.29
RI	1.67 - 1.68
Crystal	Triclinic
Properties	Strongly pleochroic
Treatments	None
Cleaning	None
Care	Warm soapy water
Composition	Complex

There are two principle sources of this highly collectable gemstone: one in the Baltistan Valley in Northern Pakistan; and one very near to K2 (the second largest mountain in the world).

Due to the difficult weather and terrain in the region, it is only possible to operate these Axinite mines for a couple of months every year. The first parcel is from a well established mine that has been producing Axinte for around 15 years.

Its colour is a breathtaking dark brown with areas of lilac when viewed from different angles: this material does have inclusions, but this allows the gem to change colour to an almost deep reddish, purple colour. The second parcel is from a fairly new mine: it is a slightly lighter brown with amazing transparency. This parcel was very difficult to get hold of as it is mined in the tribal areas along the undefined border between Afghanistan and Pakistan and my friend Shawn went to great lengths and faced real dangers in order to obtain it for me.

Discovered at the end of the 1700s, Axinite receives its name from the fact that its unusual spatula-shaped crystals are often shaped like an axe!

The reason we mention this in a gem and jewellery book, is that they were both deeply religious cultures and many of the beliefs and stories relating to the healing properties of gems originate from these civilisations.

Another reason for discussing the Aztecs is that their influence over jewellery design can still be seen in many pieces today. So fanatical were they with jewellery and gemstones that many neighbouring countries constantly worried about the threat of attack from Aztecs in search of new minerals. Not only did they craft jewellery for personal adornment and as display of authority: many would make an offering of their jewellery to their gods.

They were not just religious people, they also believed in the power of symbols and many pieces of Aztec jewellery, especially pendants and necklaces, have been unearthed where the design centres on a symbol of one kind or another.

Turquoise was incredibly popular with the Aztecs as well as several other precious stones such as Amethyst, Opals and Moonstone. Unfortunately very few gold pieces of Aztec jewellery have been preserved as much of it was melted down during the Spanish Conquest.

Aztecs

On arriving in America in the late 1400s, Spanish adventurers found two well-developed civilisations in the mid to southern regions of the country: the Incas in Peru and the often dangerous Aztec warriors of Mexico.

DID YOU KNOW?
Axis is an imaginary straight line passing through a gemstone or crystal around which its parts are systematically arranged.

AXIS

Azurite

An electric blue gemstone, like no other you will have ever seen.

Azurite is an intensely deep-blue copper mineral, which is produced by weathered copper ore deposits. It is also known as Chessylite after the name of the mine in which it was found in Lyon, France.

Historically, the gem has been set into jewellery as well as being used in Japan as a blue pigment in paintings. Azurite was also mentioned by its previous name "Kuanos" by Pliny the Elder (author and philosopher 23–79AD). Its vivid blue colour tends to diminish over time, especially when exposed to heat and light.

One of the most famous specimens of Azurite is known as the "Newmont Azurite". Originally discovered in Namibia in 1952, the gem was unusual for this variety in that it was over eight inches long. The miner who discovered it allegedly smuggled the gem out of the mine and sold it to pay off his tab at his local tavern.

We are unsure whether Azurite's name is derived from the Persian word "lazhward" or from the Arabic word "azul"; however both mean blue and this gemstone is instantly recognisable by its striking loud colour. As it is a fairly soft gemstone and one that is difficult to cut in larger sizes, it tends to be more of a collectable gemstone than one that can be worn.

The bright, vivid blues can already be seen even in its rough state.

pictures eventually fade and beautiful memories become distorted, the beauty you see in a gemstone today (as long as it is properly cared for) should last thousands of years. Many generations from now, the person that is holding your gorgeous Emerald ring, should be viewing a ring that's just as beautiful in appearance to them as it is to you. For me, gemstones offer the longest lasting form of beauty that can be possessed by man.

When we think of an object as beautiful it normally means that we are attracted to its colour, shape, style and design. But beauty in gemstones often goes deeper. The beauty derived from knowing the mystery, magic, folklore, legends and history surrounding coloured gemstones is unrivalled by any other purchasable item.

One final thought: the beauty experienced in a place, person or object often makes us feel happiness and warmth, and this feeling is amplified by our memories and past experiences. Let me give you two examples. Firstly, I find my personal gem collection grows more and more beautiful as I gain a stronger and stronger understanding about the gems. The more I research them, the better I know the myths and legends surrounding them, the more beautiful they somehow appear to me. Secondly, I believe that pieces of jewellery that have been received as a gift on special occasions and anniversaries, plus those that have been passed on from previous generations, have an additional inherent beauty.

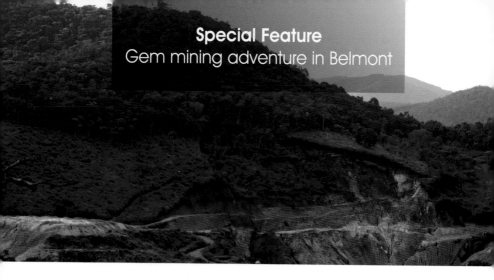

Special Feature
Gem mining adventure in Belmont

Belmont
The largest open pit mine in Brazil.

Although there are a few states in Brazil where artisanal Emerald mining is still in full swing, there is one mine operating in the Cinturao Esmeraldífe-ro ('Emerald belt') of Minas Gerais that is at the cutting edge of mining technology.

This story is set in Itabira and begins in the late 1930s when a young entrepreneur farmer, Mauro Ribeiro, started to transport diesel from Belo Horizonte (the capital city of Minais Gerias) to the local iron mines. He pushed his business hard and within just a few years had many diesel trucks travelling the route every day. He then opened his own iron mine and eventually was so successful that the authorities forcefully took over the concern and Mauro went back to farming. On his land a new railway track was built to transport the extracted minerals from the mines and many years later in 1977, whilst switching the points on the track, a young train driver spotted a green gemstone lying on the ground.

The worker took the gem to Mauro and suggested that he allowed him to take it to a nearby town where he knew gemstones were often traded. Mauro agreed and when the railroad

Owner Marcelo and Steve Bennett at the Belmont Mine .

worker returned, they shared the profits.

As Mauro already had a wealth of mining experience, it wasn't long before he was granted a licence by the government to start mining for Emeralds. Over the years the mine has had periods of strong production followed by long periods of minimal production. I met with the mine's owner Marcelo Ribeiro (Mauro's grandson) and he kindly gave us an in-depth tour of his facility.

The open pit mine is incredibly vast and is the second largest I have seen (the only one bigger is Gemfields Emerald Mine in Zambia). The top soils are a vibrant red colour formed from the Baltic rocks below. The pit is now some 300 to 400 feet deep. JCBs work at the rock face and when they hit a layer where their geologists believe there is potential of Emeralds being discovered, they scoop up all of the soil and rocks into the back of a gigantic dumper truck and the extracted minerals are taken to the sorting facility, where hopefully a green treasure or two will be found.

Marcelo explained that currently for every full dumper truck, which holds over 20 tonnes, they extract approximately 5 grams of rough Emerald of which approximately 20% is of gem quality. That's a lot of work for very few grams, especially when you consider how many thousands of tonnes of earth have already been excavated just to reach the pay dirt (pay dirt is a phrase used by miners to describe the reaching of a gem rich pocket or layer).

When you get to a certain depth in an open pit mine, if the gem rich vein continues to dip lower into the earth, there comes a point when it's no longer possible to dig any deeper. You will notice in photographs how these types of mines have big steps rising to the surface. The reason for this is that the rock faces would be unstable and liable to collapsing if they were cut vertically Therefore if at the bottom of the mine you want to dig 10 metres deeper, you need to push back and excavate soil and

Steve examining a huge rough Emerald at the Belmont mine.

rocks at every level from the top of the mine to the bottom. If you want to go deeper at the bottom of the mine, it can take as long as a year to push back each level allowing the bottom area to eventually be mined.

With so much cost involved in labour and fuel, in 2005 Marcelo decided to extend the Belmont Mine underground. Today they still operate the open pit mine, but a lot of attention and effort has gone into building a vast network of tunnels and shafts as they chase Emeralds further and further into the Earth's crust.

Before we put on our helmets and went underground to see the operation, Marcelo paused to tell me a story: In the late 1980s, his grandfather hit a pocket of Emerald that produced many grams of weight. Everyday more and more Emeralds were coming out of the ground. For a while he had more gemstones than he had customers. So he instructed the mine's manager to take all of the scree (waste from the mine) and rough rocks that they had excavated which were rich in Emeralds and to secretly cover them in earth. He was concerned that if he continued to mine so much and stored the gems that they would get stolen (theft and security is a real concern for gemstone mines all over the world). After the rich ore was covered, he instructed the miners to work on another area in the mine. Only later in a period of low yields did they return to the area where they had had a great success.

For many years the hidden rich scree and ore remained a secret of the grandfather and the mine manager. A few years ago after a period of lack-lustre performance Marcelo confided in the mine manager that he was concerned whether the mine was still viable and that if he didn't hit a good vein soon they may have to close. The mine manager, now in his late sixties, took Marcelo to one side and told him the story about his grandfather's great find and led Marcelo to where the mound of highly gem rich rock was buried.

Today Marcelo does not rely on luck in mining but uses the very latest technology in prospecting for gems. Whilst his open pit mine is the second largest I have seen, his underground mine is the most impressive I have ever had the pleasure of entering. At four metres high and five metres wide, big articulated trucks can travel through its three kilometres of tunnels.

During my visit fifteen miners and security guards were currently working the underground mine. The tunnel descends 40 metres from the height at the mine entrance and at various points the tunnel splits and weaves in several directions as miners chase an area known as the "reaction zone". The reaction zone is located alongside volcanic pegmatites that have been pushed up through cracks and crevices in the earth. The pegmatites are rich in beryllium, the building block for members of the Beryl family such as Emeralds, Aquamarine and Morganite. As the pegmatite cooled along its edge

This step feature prevents the rock collapsing under its ownweight as digging progressively gets deeper below the surface.

it picked up trace elements from the surrounding rocks and structures, in this area the rocks often had traces of chromium, which is the second building block needed for the formation of Emeralds. But that's just the foundations, for an Emerald crystal to grow it has to be exposed to the correct temperature for the right period of time; it then has to cool at a particular rate, all of this happening at the correct pressure. Of course if it wasn't this difficult, if it did not need the coming together of many elements all at the right time, then there would be gemstones aplenty. But then they wouldn't be rare and they would possess no inherent value: in fact there would then be very little separating them from manmade crystals.

Not only does Marcelo employ the latest technology in both prospecting for Emeralds and then extracting them, he uses an incredibly advanced process to sort and identify the gems. When miners are working at the rock face often they will see with their own eyes larger pieces of rough gemstones. However, identifying smaller pieces amongst tonnes of excavated rough is sometimes like looking for a needle in a haystack. In fact it's worse! At least if you are looking for a needle you have lost in a haystack, you have the encouragement of knowing it is there somewhere. When you are sifting through tonnes of rocks, pebbles and dirt in the vain hope that you might find a precious gemstone, the task becomes very difficult. Marcelo a few years ago decided to look for a solution that was less labour intensive and one that retrieved a higher percentage of

the Emeralds sporadically hidden in the rough. Traditionally miners would put the excavated material in a wire mesh pan and then swirl it around in a river to wash it and hopefully they would find a gem or two. This technique is similar to the way you may have seen images in Wild West movies where they were panning for gold. Next came big industrial washing machines that then spit out the clean rough rocks on to a conveyor belt, at which either side stood a team of eagle eyed gem sorters. But Marcelo wanted to revolutionise his operation and had heard about a technology that was used in the coffee bean industry for automatically sorting good beans from bad.

This technology is breathtaking. First the rough rocks are washed and tumbled and any obvious pieces of Emerald are removed. Next the clean rocks are spread out on a high speed conveyor belt at the end of which is a three foot drop. As the stones free-fall over the end, a set of digital cameras film them and instantly analyse their colour. If the computer spots any pieces are green it fires a series of air jets at the stone altering the direction of its fall, and blows the potential gem into a separate container. It is incredible to watch and what is even more impressive is that it has an accuracy higher than that of human gem sorters.

When it comes to the environment, Belmont take their corporate responsibilities very seriously. Rather than just pump their waste water back into the river, which is what unfortunately happens in some areas, they have designed a series of man-made filtration lakes. As each one steps down the hillside you can physically see the muddy water getting cleaner and cleaner and by the time it is pumped into the river it's good enough to drink!

I really enjoyed my time at the Belmont Mine in Itabira and would like to thank Marcelo for giving so much time to explain how his mine operated. Whilst I am a huge supporter of small artisanal miners, it is also important to appreciate the impact larger companies such as Belmont have in terms of growing the market for the wonderful coloured treasures that we all love to collect.

Bi-Coloured Tourmaline
A miracle of nature.

One of the most beautiful gemstones on the planet is the incredibly complex gemstone, Tourmaline. Just one glance at its chemical composition and all but the scientists amongst us will quickly glaze over the formula.

Colour	Several
Family	Tourmaline
Hardness	7 - 7.5
SG	3.02 - 3.1
RI	1.603 - 1.655
Crystal	Trigonal
Properties	Strong pleochroism
Treatments	Occasionally heat treated
Care	No special care needed
Composition	Very complex

So to find a piece of Tourmaline that makes the transition from one gorgeous colour to another is nothing short of a miracle of nature. But if Nature can do it once, why can't she do it twice?

Why, if Tourmaline can be found in every colour of the rainbow, can't it have several different colour combinations? There is no denying that the transition from bottle green to bubble gum pink witnessed in Bi- Coloured Tourmaline is one of the most beautiful, natural journeys on the planet, but why does it not occur with other Tourmaline colours? To find out the answer to this question I quizzed Brazilian gem expert Joas Salvador.

Joas explained that it's not impossible to find Bi-Coloured Tourmalines that feature other colours, in fact over the years Joao explained that there had been a fair amount that traverse from a brown to green colour, but these had not been coming out of the ground in recent times. Other combinations

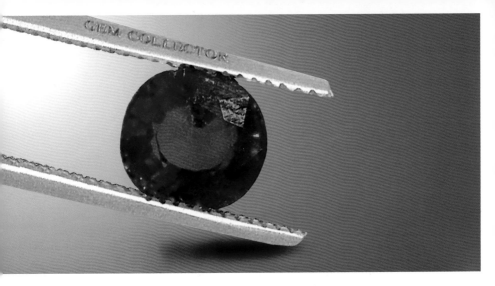

Also known as Red Emerald and Scarlet Emerald, Bixbite is regarded by many as the rarest member of the Beryl family. The gem is named in honour of the legendary mineralogist Maynard Bixby (1853 – 1935) of Utah, America, who was believed to have first discovered the gem in 1904.

Many gems marketed as Bixbite are in fact a different gem known as Pezzottaite. The confusion arises as both their chemical construction and appearance are almost identical. Bixbite, however, is currently only mined in two locations on the planet: the Wah Wah Mountains in Utah, America, and in the Catron and Sierra Counties, New Mexico. Pezzottaite, on the other hand, was first discovered in Madagascar in 2002. Although the mines are now said to be depleted, luckily there has been a recent discovery in Afghanistan.

Manganese causes the gem's stunning red appearance, and although the gem is often heavily included and at best translucent, many collectors regard the gem as a greater acquisition than Ruby. The most covetable colour is a deep pink. Unfortunately over the past few years, we have not been able to source the gem in any reasonable quantity.

Bixbite

or Pezzottaite? These two gemstones are often confused.

Colour	Orangey red, red, purple red
Family	Beryl
Hardness	7.5 – 8.0
SG	2.66 – 2.70
RI	1.567 – 1.580
Crystal	Hexagonal
Properties	None
Treatments	Colourless oil and resin
Care	No special care needed
Cleaning	Warm soapy water
Composition	$Be_3(AlMn)_2Si_6O_{18}$

Black Diamonds are a stunning and very fashionable variety of Diamond. Although it lacks dispersion and the internal brilliance of its colourless sister, a quality Black Diamond has the ability to display an intense surface lustre, with an almost metallic shimmer.

Black Diamond
Highly fashionable, with incredible lustre and unparalleled scintillation.

Natural Black Diamonds are extremely hard and beautiful, and are found predominantly in Africa. As with all Diamonds, they were formed in the earth many millions of years ago and have been pushed to the Earth's surface by volcanic eruptions.

Black Diamonds have become increasingly popular in recent years. Although not strictly black, they contain numerous dark inclusions that give this Diamond its characteristic black look. Many Black Diamonds undergo treatment to intensify the blackness of their colour. When buying Black Diamonds it's best to always assume they have been treated, especially if they are a true jet black colour. As the only optical effect we are looking for in Black Diamonds is lustre and scintillation, a buyer's main focus should be on the quality of its surface. For the gem to perform properly, it is imperative that it has been well cut and polished that it is free of major defects such as pits, cracks and crevices.

Colour	Black
Family	Diamond
Hardness	10
SG	3.5
Ri	2.41
Crystal	Cubic
Properties	Strong lustre
Treatments	Normally irradiated
Care	No special care needed
Cleaning	Ultrasonic, steam cleaning or warm soapy water
Composition	C (Carbon)

Black Gems & Associations

A classic colour chosen by jewellery wearers of all ages.

Black is the ultimate dark colour that conveys elegance, although strictly speaking it is not truly a colour at all. Black gems, as with any object that is black, do not reflect any visible light.

Coloured gemstones obtain their colour by the way their atoms absorb and reflect different colours of the spectrum.

A red gem, such as a Ruby, absorbs all of the green and blue colours of the spectrum and reflects only the red rays, while colourless gemstones such as Diamonds and Zircon reflect all colours of the spectrum. Black gems on the other hand, absorb all colours and therefore none are reflected back to the eye.

In ancient times, when men wore black they were said to have good sense and fortitude, while single women wearing the colour were said to be fickle and foolish (don't shoot the messenger! I'm just quoting ancient history: when women wear black today they are not foolish at all, quite the opposite). When married women wore the colour however, it stood for perseverance and constant love. The colour was also associated with Saturdays and the planet Saturn.

Black is also the colour of rebellion, which could be true in the gem world as there are so few gems that are naturally black; indeed, these could be deemed as nature's rebellions. Only a handful of gems found on Earth are naturally true black: Jet, Haematite and Black Spinel – although the latter is very rare indeed. Black Onyx is actually a Chalcedony, which has been dyed using a technique that is over 2000 years old. The black gem Tektite was created millions of years ago when a meteorite fell to earth and morphed with rocks on the surface of the earth to create one of the few out-of-space gems. Natural Black Diamonds are rarely strictly black, as they nearly always feature dark inclusions which create an appearance similar to that of a black raven feather with a shimmering black lustre.

Bleeding

The draining of a colour in a gemstone due to lighting conditions is known as bleeding.

Not a nice thought, but this is the best way I can think of describing it: you know how you tend to lose colour when you badly cut yourself? Well, that is what we mean when we say that a gemstone bleeds. Now of course a gemstone cannot bleed in the same sense, but if you view a gem under one light source and then under another some gems will suffer the same effect. Bleeding is not be confused with the effect known as "colour change" where a totally different hue is seen, it's more to do with the draining of colour.

For example most Sapphires when worn in doors under incandescent light can often lack sparkle; their tone seems to diminish and the gem almost fades, but once taken back outside into natural sunlight their tone is instantly revitalised. Not all Sapphires bleed in the same way and the level of their bleeding depends on their chemical composition.

Garnets and Tourmalines are also prone to bleeding and it is for this reason that at Gems TV, we first show our jewellery under studio incandescent lighting so that their "bled colour" can be seen and then,

Natural fancy-coloured Diamonds are amongst the most expensive and valuable of all gemstones. Coloured Diamonds, especially Blue Diamonds, are becoming increasingly popular with collectors and celebrities.

Nothing quite matches a Blue Diamond in colour: being comparable to a crossbreed of the deepest London Blue Topaz and darkest Santa Maria Aquamarine, it really does have a uniqueness all of its own.

Highly prized, natural Blue Diamonds are exceptionally rare and historically could cost up to 20 times more than White Diamonds of the same clarity and carat weight. Today to obtain their vibrant blue colour, most Blue Diamonds on the market are heat treated and/or irradiated. That said, they still often demand a higher price than a colourless Diamond of an equivalent grade.

Most Blue Diamonds will have a slight greyish mask affecting their colour saturation and those with a tone of around 80 to 85% seem to appear the most beautiful, as they are open enough to still demonstrate brilliance and dispersion. Without doubt the most famous Blue Diamond of all time is the 45.2ct Hope Diamond.

Blue Diamond

is said to be the second most expensive substance on earth, only surpassed by natural Red Diamonds!

Blue Gems and Associations

The hottest selling colour of gemstone so far this century.

Reputedly the most popular male colour, blue promotes calmness and tranquillity and is aesthetically perceived as a cool colour. It lowers the heart rate and breathing, and is also believed to suppress appetite.

When a man wears blue he is said to be wise and thoughtful; a lady in blue is said to be polite and vigilant. The colour is associated with Friday and the planet Venus.

When it comes to blue gems there are several to choose from, the most famous being Sapphire. Although today Sapphires have been discovered in many different hues, historically it was believed that the only colour Sapphires could be found in was blue. It is for this reason that when the word Sapphire is used without a colour prefix, it is always assumed to be blue.

Since its discovery in 1967, Tanzanite has now become possibly the most sought after of all blue gemstones.

If you are looking for a light blue gem with great clarity, then March's birthstone, Aquamarine, might be your preferred choice. Topaz is another gem that is available in blue and is given different prefixes, dependent on its tone. Sky Blue Topaz is the name given to the

Deep, vivid blues of London Blue Topaz.

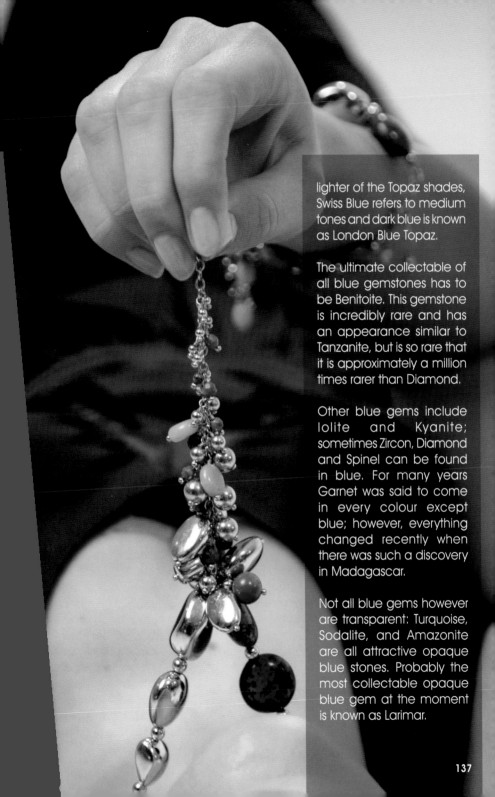

lighter of the Topaz shades, Swiss Blue refers to medium tones and dark blue is known as London Blue Topaz.

The ultimate collectable of all blue gemstones has to be Benitoite. This gemstone is incredibly rare and has an appearance similar to Tanzanite, but is so rare that it is approximately a million times rarer than Diamond.

Other blue gems include Iolite and Kyanite; sometimes Zircon, Diamond and Spinel can be found in blue. For many years Garnet was said to come in every colour except blue; however, everything changed recently when there was such a discovery in Madagascar.

Not all blue gems however are transparent: Turquoise, Sodalite, and Amazonite are all attractive opaque blue stones. Probably the most collectable opaque blue gem at the moment is known as Larimar.

Blue Moonstone Quartz

Unique, intriguing and so far only found in one deposit.

One of the most intriguing discoveries in Brazil over the past 10 years is the small deposit of Blue Moonstone Quartz in one of the oldest gemstone mines in South Brazil. Some 30 feet underground in a small area known as "The Urugaena", a thin seam of slightly grey Quartz was discovered. 'At first it didn't look that exciting underground', says the mine owner; 'However when it was brought to the surface it had the appearance like that of a cross between Moonstone and Blue Fire Opal, it's truly a real treasure and a heavenly gemstone.'

Colour	Whitish Blue
Family	Quartz
Hardness	7
SG	2.66
RI	1.5 - 1.55
Crystal	Hexagonal
Treatments	Heat
Care	None
Cleaning	Ultrasonic or warm soapy water
Composition	SiO_2

My good friends who facet this gemstone for me tell me that to get the very best out of the gemstone and to maximise its mystical Moonstone-like glow, you have to be very patient when studying the rough, being sure to view it from every single angle before making the first cut. Get it right and the gemstone is truly beautiful, get it wrong and it just doesn't have the same gorgeous, almost magical appearance. Blue Moonstone Quartz has so far only been discovered in Brazil and locals believe that the gemstone instils and nurtures love. This is a must have gemstone for all collectors.

Blue Sapphire
Fit for a princess.

Blues are still amongst the most popular and sought after type of Sapphire and have been the prized possessions of emperors, kings, queens and collectors for thousands of years. Of all the coloured gemstones it is possibly the most renowned and demanded. Royalty have been known to give Sapphires over Diamonds as engagement rings because they are known to be far rarer than the latter. The most notable producer of fine Blue Sapphires is Sri Lanka and it is often referred to by its previous name, Ceylon Sapphire.

Colour	Pale blue to deep rich midnight blue
Family	Corundum
Hardness	9
SG	3.9 – 4.1
RI	1.76 – 1.77
Crystal	Trigonal
Properties	Strong pleochroism
Treatments	Normally heat treated
Cleaning	Ultrasonic, Steam Cleaning or Warm soapy Water
Care	No special care needed
Composition	Al_2O_3

As Sapphire is renowned for being blue, when the word is used without a colour prefix, it is assumed that one is talking about Blue Sapphire. All other colours are regarded as "fancy Sapphires" and should be prefixed with their colour. Just as in the wine world it is improper to say Chardonnay Chablis, it would be equally wrong to say Blue Sapphire when describing the Blue variety: being politically correct you simply say, Sapphire.

Evaluating Sapphires
The most attractive Sapphires are those that are a pure blue. Whilst pure body colours are desirable in most gemstones, those whose colour is a primary colour

such as the red of Rubies and the blue of Sapphire, really can demand a price premium when their hue is pure. That said, some gem collectors prefer their Blue Sapphires to have a 10 to 15% purple mix within the gem's colour.

In terms of saturation you will sometimes see a greyish mask (see mask heading in Volume II to get a better handle on saturation and masks) and if the gem lacks life this could be the cause. In terms of tone it depends on your preference between lighter cornflower blues and deeper royal blues. Unfortunately today we see far too many Sapphires on the market, especially from some locals in China and Australia, where the tone is almost 100% (i.e. black).

Another important evaluation criterion for both members of the corundum family (Sapphire and Ruby) is whether the gem bleeds or not (see bleeding heading). When some Sapphires are worn indoors under incandescent light, they can often lack sparkle, their tone seems to diminish and the gem almost fades, but take them back outside and they instantly revitalise. Not all Sapphires bleed in the same way and the level of their bleeding depends on their chemical composition.

Probably more than any other gem (with the exception maybe of Pearls), Sapphires have often been valued more for their origin than their beauty. But to paraphrase the most legendary of all gem explorers ever, George Kunz, great gemstones can be found in any location and poor ones can be unearthed at locales that are renowned

for the most highly prized. You are just as likely to find a poor quality Sapphire in Kashmir as a stunner in China.

The key evaluation criteria for Sapphire, as with all coloured gems, remain the vividness of its colour, its transparency, its clarity, its cut, etc. Then of course, if you are faced with a choice of two similar gemstones from different locales, you might choose to acquire the one with an origin that is renowned for producing great pieces of that gem variety, or you may even choose the other piece that is the shining star of an under-rated locale.

Let's discuss the properties that are typically associated with each location, but please do bear in mind the above comments. These are the summary of the huge amount of books I have read, yet my own experience is more in line with the views of George Kunz in that quality and appearance can vary from location to location.

My opinion, that it is not wise to generalise about locales, is based primarily on viewing the gems that flow through my sorting office in Jaipur and those that we sell through our various channels. It is also based on the fact that when I was recently in Zambia I witnessed from one small location in a mine, no bigger than three foot square, a miner unearth the most stunning, clear deep green Emerald, only five minutes later to find two more pieces that were dull and lifeless. The difference can be narrowed even further: it's not just the country, the region, the particular mine, the area within the mine that makes a difference, but the portion of the rough that your gem has been cut from. Only yesterday I was in my cutting facility where we were cutting some of the finest Amethyst rough we have ever purchased: after making the first slice (a slice is the first cut made to gemstone rough, performed to remove a part of a gem with a big fracture or large feather inclusion), we were left with two totally different grades.

So the information below is more related to the typical types of Sapphires found in each location. It's more like saying you will find more Brits in Britain, more Thais in Thailand and more Indians in India. But if you look in today's cosmopolitan cities, you will realise this type of view is no longer completely valid. It is also important to point out that with today's modern gemstone treatments, such as colour diffusion, these differences are less reliable than they used to be in terms of arriving at a dependable origin, based on appearance alone.

Kashmir Sapphires

Regarded by many as the finest Sapphires in the world, they were first discovered in 1879 in the Padar region of Kashmir in Northern India after a landslip allegedly uncovered their occurrence. The Kashmir Sapphire has been known for over a century as "the Jewel of India". Unfortunately, after just a few years of mining, the area became unworkable due to the deposit being in the middle of a politically unstable area and one fraught with conflict. The matter worsened in 1947 after the partition of the subcontinent, and Kashmir, which is located in the Himalayas some 4500 metres above sea level, has been war torn ever since. So whether it is a result of the conflict or the fact that the mine was depleted within just a few years of its discovery is still not completely understood and remains one of the most talked about topics in gem circles.

Even though the driving force behind its true rarity is not known, at an auction at Christie's in 2007 a 22.66 carat Kashmir Sapphire set in a gold pendant fetched a price of $3,064,000. This equates to around £85,000 per carat!

Kashmir Sapphires are renowned world wide for their almost sleepy appearance. The reason for this is that they have thousands of microscopic inclusions: these cannot be seen by the naked eye, but under a microscope can normally be identified. Also known as flour, these inclusions diffuse the light, providing the Sapphire with its legendary sleepy appearance. The Kashmir Sapphire typically is a very pure blue, with few secondary colours and has a medium tone of 70 to 80%.

Ceylon Sapphire

Made famous in the UK after Princess Diana was given a large Ceylon Sapphire in the centre of her engagement ring and subsequently

Christ the Redeemer, Rio de Janeiro, Brazil.

to the world's supply of gemstones by volume, it is estimated that a quarter of all faceted gems in the world each year originate from Brazil. That's quite amazing when you consider that three of the largest selling gemstones, Diamonds, Rubies and Sapphires, are only mined on a very small scale.

According to official data supplied by the IBGM (Brazilian Agency for the Promotion of Export and Investment) just four out of the 26 states in Brazil are responsible for 97% of its gemstone production, namely Minas Gerais, Mato Grosso, Bahia and Rio Grande do Sul.

Minas Gerais

Gemstone mining is so important in terms of the economy in this state, that even its name means General Mining. It's impossible to know for sure how many people are involved in the mining industry in Minas Gerais, as due to very high taxation on gemstones, much of the mining is carried out illegally. However, IBGM state that over 100 companies are involved in official mining and over 300 companies are cutting and polishing gemstones. It is believed that as many as 170,000 families have their income supported by gemstone activities in this one region alone!

The State of Minas Gerais can then be broken down into seven important geological regions:

- Pedra Azul for Topaz and Aquamarine.
- Padre Paraiso where Aquamarine, Chrysoberyl, Helidor and Topaz can be found.

- Conselheiro Pena for Tourmaline, Aquamarine, Morganite and Kunzite.

- Santa Maria de Itabira where Emerald, Alexandrite and Aquamarine of incredible quality have been unearthed.

- Sao Jose da Safira for Tourmaline, Morganite and Garnet.

- Malacacheta for Chrysoberyl including its colour change variety Alexandrite.

- Aracuai for Tourmaline, Aquamarine, Morganite and Topaz.

In most of these gem bearing districts, the finds are normally associated with granitic rocks and hydrothermal deposits.

In addition to those already mentioned, Minas Gerais also yields small pockets of Hiddenite, Scapolite, Brazilianite, Petalite, Amblygonite and low grade Ruby and Sapphire.

Bahia

Although Minas Gerais produces more cut gemstones than the state of Bahia, in terms of gemstone rough, Bahia is second only to Rio Grande do Sul. Much of the gem trading is conducted in Salvador and the rough is then normally sent to cities such

Brazil: a gemstone treasure chest.

as Jaipur for cutting and polishing. Some of the most important gems in the region are Emerald, Amethyst and Aquamarine. But how about the following for a treasure chest: Alexandrite, Amazonite, Andalusite, Apatite, Chrysoberyl, Citrine, Diamond, Dumortierite, Emerald, Fluorite, Jasper, Malachite, Morganite, Ruby, Rutile Quartz, Sapphire, Topaz, Tourmaline, Turquoise and Zircon have also been discovered.

During the 19th century many Diamond prospectors were busy mining in a region known as Chapa Diamantina. In an attempt to protect the beautiful National Park in Chapa, in 1996 the government placed a ban on Diamond mining and now Bahia is all about colour!

Now here is a bit of trivia: where are some of the world's oldest Emeralds discovered? Well Emeralds in the famous Swat Valley in Pakistan are estimated to be around just 23 million years old (very young in gem terms),

those from Chivor and other areas in Colombia date back to around 65 million years ago. Prior to that, Emeralds in the Minas Gerais and Santa Terezinha in Goias were formed approximately 500 million years ago. However, in Carnaiba and Socoto in the state of Bahia, Emeralds were formed around 2 billion years ago! That's old!

Rio Grande Do Sul

For Agate and Amethyst, Rio Grande do Sul (the most southern state in Brazil) is the most important gemstone location on the planet and over 90% of the state's gemstone revenue is derived from these. Rio Grande do Sul is also the largest gemstone mining state in Brazil and most of the gem trading is done in the municipality of Soledade.

Much of the world's supply of Citrine is also mined here, however it comes out of the ground as Amethyst, which is then heat treated and the high concentration of iron found naturally in the gems from this region oxidise, turning the gem an incredible glowing sunflower yellow.

Mato Grosso & Goias

Made famous for its discovery of Emerald in the northern region of the state in 1981, Mato Grosso also has small deposits of Diopside, Garnet and Zircon.

Over the past few decades, the Santa Terezinha mines in the state of Goias have provided some of the most important sources of Emerald in Brazil. Unfortunately, the Santa Terezinha mine, from which Coloured Rocks sourced its beautiful Emeralds from in early 2010, is no longer in production. These Emeralds exhibit a greenish dark blue/yellowish pale green pleochroism which is characteristic of their distinguished beauty. Emeralds by their very nature are prone to natural inclusions, so look out for the occasional 'Terezinha Black Spot': the local miners claim it brings good fortune and good luck!

In addition to the four big mining states of Brazil, there are two more worthy of a mention:

Paraiba

Even if they have never seen it firsthand, there is not a gem dealer worth his salt that will not at least have heard of Paraiba Tourmaline. The gem received its name as it was first discovered in 1988 in the state of Paraiba in a region known as Mina da Batalha.

Unfortunately, very little Paraiba Tourmaline has ever been discovered in Paraiba and very few pieces from the initial find weigh over half a carat! Today, for Paraiba Tourmaline we have to turn to Mozambique to discover the gem, but these deposits have all but dried up too! Unless new sources of Paraiba Tourmaline are discovered, I would like to suggest a very beautiful alternative from the state of Paraiba: Amblygonite. Not only is the gemstone found in the same region, visually it is strikingly similar: demonstrating a blend of swimming pool blues and sea green hues.

Piaui

Pronounced 'pee-Ow-Ee'.

The Opals from this region as a general rule tend to be more 'pinfire' as opposed to 'broadflash'. If you are new to this gem terminology, basically speaking 'pinfire' is, as its name suggests, the appearance of multi coloured pin sized spots appearing across the Opal as it moves. In Piaui Opals it is more common to see this type of effect rather than 'broadflash', where the colours tend to flow into one another like water over an oily surface.

As well as unearthing Opals looking similar to their Australian counterpart, Piaui is also home to some wonderful Fire Opals. During 1997 there was even a discovery of Blue Fire Opal in the state.

After Australia, Brazil is probably the

Extinct Amethyst mine converted into huge wine cellar.

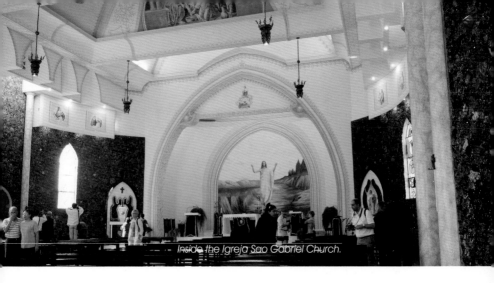
Inside the Igreja Sao Gabriel Church.

be it of a low commercial grade) to line the entire walls of the church. It was breathtakingly beautiful. Matt - my son and cameraman - asked if I could do a spontaneous piece for the documentary we were filming during our trip, but for once I had to tell him to just sit back and soak up the experience; it was mesmerising. For centuries Amethyst has had a close link with the Catholic Church and here was the Igreja Sao Gabriel Church completely lined with rough cut gems. The altar was even a huge geode, the font used for baptism was also a geode, and the back of the priest's chair was two huge Amethysts flanking a row of Citrine.

The next day we travelled to Soledade, to meet Mr Agate: that's not his real name of course but Mauricio Lodi runs one of the largest Agate cutting and treatment companies on the planet. All of his gems come from near the banks of the beautiful "Salto do Jacui"; this remote location is famed for producing some of the finest patterned Agates available anywhere. Most of the Agates formed at this location are inside miniature geodes with sizes rarely exceeding two feet. Many of them completely fill the geode, whilst others come to rest with a small hole in the centre which is often lined with Drusy. Over the time I spent with Mauricio, I can honestly say that I saw every natural colour possible across the collection of Agates he had in stock. However, as the hues, tones and saturation varied in every single piece, many are dyed to provide the gem with a more saturated and repeatable colour.

Mauricio explained how each colour uses a different treatment; his blues and greens were dyed at a temperature in excess of 200 degrees and the colour was permanent. Pinks and purples however had to be dyed at lower temperatures and he warned that if left in exposed sunlight for excessive periods they would fade slightly. I thought this was worthy as a mention just in case I ever started selling his outdoor

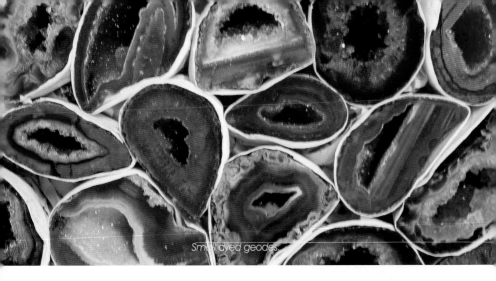

Agate wind charms! The colours of the dyes have intense saturation and yet somehow the patterns are not masked, but appear to be more defined.

As well as being possibly the world's largest supplier of Agates, Mauricio is also known as Mr. Geode. His geode production is incredible, with some pieces being over ten feet tall and one piece I saw weighed over three tonnes! If you ever visit Gems TV's UK television studios, the two huge pieces in our reception were sawn and prepared by one of Mauricio's skilled employees. For more information on geodes see the section later on in this book.

Whilst I was in the area I met up with Joe an old friend of mine whose business partner had discovered a new Fire Opal in the area and asked if I wanted to buy their run of mine (a run of mine is effectively a commitment to take whatever they extract over a period of time and at a set price). The colours were amazing, the clarity

The famous Iguaçu waterfall.

was as good as I have seen from Mexico and therefore I agreed to take everything they currently had in inventory.

Next we went to do a spot of sightseeing at the famous Iguaçu waterfalls. These are situated at the border between Paraguay, Brazil and Argentina and are without doubt one of the most mesmerising landscapes on planet Earth. After seeing the falls from the Brazilian side we crossed the border into Argentina to film from the other side. This was even more breathtaking. After a day of chilling it was back to business and Matt and I flew to Bel Horizona the capital of Minas Gerais to go to a barbecue being held by gem expert Marcelo Bernardes at which many important members of the ICA were attending.

The next morning we decided to split up: Matt would go and film with my good buddy Glenn Lehrer at the world's most famous Imperial Topaz mine at Ouro Preto, and I would fly to Minas Gerais and spend one day sourcing gems in Valaderes and one day in Tefino Antoni. These two neighbouring towns (well, one hundred miles is pretty much a neighbour in Brazil) are the country's equivalent of Jaipur, India Bangkok, and Thailand when it comes to the trading, cutting and exporting of gemstones. A very good friend of mine, Joas Salvador, was going to take care of me for my two day visit. The first day I spent looking at a parcel of Morganite that Joas Salvador had treated for us then applied the first cut which is known as a "preform". Let me explain this in a little more detail: Joas had been collecting the rough from a particular mine in Mozambique for around one year. It was then sent to Brazil where Joas Salvador's team sliced and preformed the gem. A preform cut provides the gemstone with its outline shape.

As this collection was of a very high grade, Joas Salvador decided to send the parcel to a laboratory in Thailand to have it irradiated. Next it was shipped

Imperial Topaz mine at Ouro Preto.

back to Brazil to undergo its final heat treatment. That's a lot of travelling and expense, but when you deal with fine quality gemstones, it's worth making sure that the end result is the best you can get. Many cutting houses don't perform the final heat treating process, but without it I am told the colour of the Morganite becomes unstable.

I sat with Joas and negotiated a deal for his entire collection: whilst he was happy with the hard price I bargained, he did say that it would not be repeatable in the future, as the price of the rough had gone through the roof due to increased demand for the gemstone in Asia, and also there had been a steep rise in the cost of mining. So we sealed the parcel, filled in all of the complex export paperwork and prepared them for shipping to our cutting house in Jaipur. This is the exciting part for me and also the big gamble: I have to estimate what the end carat weight will be after we have faceted the gems. Whilst it is a little easier buying preforms than buying

the rough straight from the mine, (where your yield can be anywhere from 3% to 50%), as Morganite is an expensive gem if my yield is less than 65% then my calculations on value become incorrect and will most likely lose money.

So when you next see one of our beautiful Mozambique Morganites, just think how much work has gone into first prospecting for the gem, then mining it, then preforming, heating, irradiating and once again heating, and that's all before one of our highly skilled lapidarists even cuts the first facet.

Next, Joas was excited to show me a brand new discovery from the North of Brazil at an area known as the Para estate, close to the mine Sao Geraldo do Araguaia. As he opened up his woven grey sack in which he kept his samples from the mine, the sunlight caught the top of one of the crystals and I saw golden snowflakes in an ice cube. Well not quite, this was a transparent quartz that had two

A cut piece of Bi-Coloured Tourmaline resting on a fresh piece of uncut rough.

mineral inclusions trapped inside, the most abundant I am sure is Pyrite and the second inclusion, we are going to have to wait until I get a laboratory report to correctly identify. Joas needed some cash to go back and carry on extracting the gem and I agreed to underpin his next round of mining.

The next morning I visited Saint Clair Fonseca Jûnior, he is one of the most well known miners in Minas Gerais. Saint-Clair specialises in prospecting and then extracting Tourmalines, not just in Brazil but also in Mozambique. We sat and discussed his mining operation and I asked him what pockets, (an area in a mine where gems are found), his team had found recently.

Saint-Clair took the key to the safe, disappeared for a couple of minutes and returned with a small parcel of bi-coloured Tourmaline. Each piece had really nice transparency and when I mentioned this, Saint-Clair said he had one small parcel that was even better a few weeks before, but the Chinese

buyers arrived and bought the entire production: at a staggering price of over a thousand dollars per carat! That was certainly a new benchmark for this stone as far as I was concerned, but later in the trip I spoke to one miner who told me the Chinese were now paying up to $2000 for top grade Bi- Coloured Tourmaline.

Whilst the parcel I was looking at was indeed beautiful, as Saint-Clair and myself believe in long term mutually beneficial business relationships he offered me a very good price. I was extremely happy as I had not been able to source any really nice quality Bi-Coloured Tourmaline for over three years. He asked if I would like to film at his mining operation whilst I was in the area and we agreed to visit later in the week once Matt had rejoined me.

Next he asked if I wanted to see the biggest Morganite in the world: I told him that would not be possible as to my knowledge I already owned the largest piece. Saint-Clair smiled, walked over

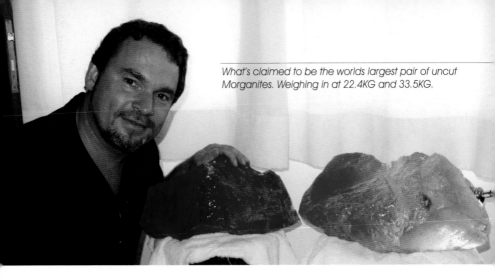

What's claimed to be the worlds largest pair of uncut Morganites. Weighing in at 22.4KG and 33.5KG.

to the side of his office where there were two small wooden stools with large dishcloths covering something resting on top. Like a magician revealing a rabbit at the end of a trick, Saint-Clair whipped off the cloth and I froze to the spot. Speechless, unable to comprehend what lay before me, were two huge pieces of rough Morganite. The colour was amazing, the size was unimaginable and once I took a lamp to it, I could see that it was a fairly clean crystal. The larger piece weighed 33.5KG. I asked Saint-Clair if they had been treated in anyway, he told me that when he first got the stones the colour was not as beautiful, so he left them outside in his back yard for a couple of months and through the natural radiation of the sun, the pieces transformed into the vivid colour they now are.

I asked what he was going to do with them and he said that our mutual friend Glenn had made an offer for one of the pieces at the Tucson Gem Show back in January and I recommended that this was probably the most likely home for them. Glenn is one of the world's leading gemstone carvers and I said that I could just imagine the sort of design he could do. If Glenn didn't purchase them I suggested Saint-Clair maybe offer them to a museum.

Before I left I asked him why nobody was unearthing any Paraiba Tourmaline in Mozambique, Saint-Clair said that they had recently found a new pocket at his mine and the quality was superb, "would you like to see a few pieces" he asked, "is the Pope Catholic?" I responded. Wow, these pieces were perfect, possessing great clarity and a text book swimming pool colour. Then the bad news, Saint-Clair was asking two thousand dollars a carat: I tried to negotiate but he was not even entertaining the idea of dropping his price. I asked why the price had soared and once again the answer was the same as I had been hearing all year long, there is a huge demand in Asia right now for this treasure also.

The view over the Doce Valley

The stones were exceptional though, but in these situations as a gem buyer I have to make sure my head over rules my heart. Also as one of the larger buyers in the market, it's important that I don't set a precedent with miners, if I had shown any remote interest when he mentioned the price, news would have spread around the industry that we were entertaining the idea of paying the new prices higher.

A gemstone buyer negotiating with a miner is like two people playing poker: neither reveals their hand. Sometimes the seller starts incredibly high to judge the buyer's reaction, sometimes the buyer starts ridiculously low to get the game started. All of the time both parties commenting on the quality of the goods; the seller always claiming that it is an exceptionally good price for the quality he has on offer, always saying that the gems are getting harder to find and how his cost of mining is ever going up, the buyer arguing how his customers will not pay the price and therefore he cannot buy it anywhere

near the price the seller wants. Always both players leave the door open by not making any absolute claims. But in this instance I could sense Saint-Clair was very serious about the price, so I said I was not going to even make an offer. "OK Steve, why don't I invite you out to the mine in Mozambique, you can come and film and see for yourself how little is coming out of the ground and then maybe you might start increasing your offers a little". Going into a Paraiba mine, with one of the industry's leading experts on the gem, was an offer I could not refuse and we hope to make the trip sometime during the summer.

That afternoon Joas and I left Valaderes and drove northeast for approximately 100 miles to the town of Teofilo Otoni (pronounced Tee-af-alo Otoni). The road was similar to an English A road in width, but that is where the similarity ended. It twisted and wound along beautiful rolling scenery, the volcanic red soil which can be seen across virtually the entire south of Brazil

Matt filming in the gemstone village of São José da Safira

providing the perfect base for huge green forests to flourish. Teofilo Otoni is a very important gem town in Minas Gerais and an area where many of the locally mined Aquamarines, Emeralds, Alexandrites, Tourmalines and Chrysoberyl are traded.

Joas had arranged with a friend of his to use his office for the afternoon and had already put the word out on the street that I would be coming to town to source gems. By the time we had arrived, there was already a long line of gem miners, cutters and traders waiting to try and sell their goods. This is very similar to the way we often buy in Jaipur, however the queue was much more orderly than in India. One other difference is these people were not the principles. In India it's normally the actual owner of the gems that arrives to sell his stones, even if they have to queue for four hours, a sale makes it worth their while. In Teofilo Otoni owners tend to send someone to display their gems for them so that they don't have to waste an afternoon

in a line! It's a little frustrating though as all deals need a phone call to the owner to see if they accept the offer.

I saw around 60 to 70 deals over the afternoon and we sealed the final one at around 8pm and started our two hour drive back to Valadares. One of the main gems I was looking for was Indicolite: unfortunately nobody had more than a dozen pieces in a single parcel. This was a little frustrating as I only managed to find 27 pieces over a six hour buying session. I did however get a few amazing deals on Aquamarine and a very nice pair of matching pear cut Paraiba Tourmalines.

The next morning Joas drove me three hours to the Belmont Emerald Mine, I arrived at 9am and met up with the owner Marcelo Ribeiro. He explained the history behind the mine, which was first started by his grandfather Mauro Ribeiro in 1979.

The Belmont mine is probably the second largest open pit coloured

Travelling to work 'São José Da Safira' style

gem mine on the planet and their underground mine is certainly the largest I have ever visited. The mine is located in an Emerald-rich region called Itabira and incredibly well managed, with state of the art equipment. For more details on this mine see the Belmont mine feature. Friday morning we woke early: it was the last day of our Brazilian adventure and we had saved the best until last. This is the day we were going to visit Saint-Clair's Pederneira Mine and the most important Tourmaline deposit of the past 40 years at the Cruzeiro Mine.

Once you leave the main road outside of Valaderes you have to travel around 70 miles on a very bumpy dust track to reach the Tourmaline-rich pegmatites. The track is so rough that it took us over three hours to reach our destination, although we didn't mind too much as the scenery was spectacular with cattle farms and ranches set into the hillside along virtually the entire journey.

Before we arrived at the mines, we stopped at a little village called São José Da Safira, here for many years gemstones from the surrounding hill sides have been traded. Joas told me, "I was born and raised in the village,

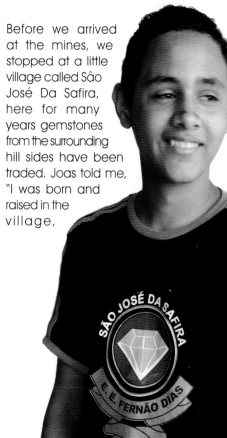

The colourful village life at Safira

most gem trading gets done on a Friday so that the miners have enough money to buy food for their families for the weekend". It's a really quaint place; as we arrived the local school were on their lunch break and all of the children

were wearing the school tee-shirt which had a huge sketch of a gemstone in the centre. All the houses were painted bright vivid colours to represent the various colours that Tourmaline can be found, and being a Friday we could

sense an air of anticipation of deals that would be done that afternoon. As we were leaving the village we saw two miners bringing their rough gemstones into the village in sacks hanging from the saddles of their horse.

Within just a mile or so from the village you start your ascent into the mountains. The road turns back into a bumpy dust road after a brief but welcome spell of tarmac through the village. As you climb, the views across the valley continue to grow more beautiful. It's exactly the image I had had in my head of what I thought the Brazilian countryside would look like. Dense forests, thick under-growth and the relaxing sounds of crickets made the ordeal of our journey pass more quickly, however I was starting to feel slightly bruised from bouncing up and down for three hours and constantly banging myself as I tried to capture the scenery through my camera lens. We finally arrived at the Pederneira Mine and Saint-Clair was there to meet us. He first of all showed us around the

Miner's village near the Pedreneira mine

"So my time in Brazil was over. I had met many amazing gem experts along the way, visited the most important Tourmaline deposits in the world and even spent several days having a go at gem mining for myself.

Brazil is undoubtedly one of the most diverse gem mining countries I have visited and it won't be long before I return on my next gem hunting adventure."

Breastplate of Aaron

It is believed that the tradition of birthstones arose from the Breastplate of Aaron, a ceremonial religious garment that was set with twelve gemstones.

The gems represented the twelve tribes of Israel, which also corresponded with the twelve signs of the zodiac and the twelve months of the year.

It is referred to in the book of Exodus in the Old Testament of the Bible and was made for Moses' brother Aaron and his sons to be worn as a garment so they could serve as priests.

Taken from Exodus: "It is to be square – a span long and a span wide and folded double. Then mount four rows of precious stones on it. In the first row there shall be a Ruby, a Topaz and a Beryl; in the second row a Turquoise, a Sapphire and an Emerald; in the third row a Jacinth, an Agate and an Amethyst; in the fourth row a Chrystolite, an Onyx and a Jasper". (28:16-17).

The Breastplate of Aaron is of interest to gem lovers as it is an early account of the use of gemstones as both decoration and symbolism. The breastplate is described in the Bible as the "Breastplate of Judgement" or the "Breastplate of Decision". As they used ancient biblical descriptions for the gems, unfortunately it is difficult for translators to determine several of those used with exact certainty. Therefore, the list of gems varies slightly depending on which translation is used.

The Bronze Age can be split into three periods; Early Bronze Age (3500-2200 BC), Middle Bronze Age (2200-1550 BC), and Late Bronze Age (1550-1200 BC).

Metalsmiths in the Bronze Age developed an astonishingly high level of skill in bronze and gold working and used twisting and forging methods to make wrist and neck torques.

Towards the final stages of the Early Bronze Age and the start of the Middle Bronze Age, a new type of jewellery appeared in the Budapest region. This new jewellery included rings which were not complete bands as they are today, but instead had twisted ends. Other types of jewellery included spiral necklaces, and corkscrew and half-moon styled earrings. The spread of jewellery along the Danube area helps confirm the formation of the trade route of the Early Bronze Age. From this jewellery, mostly found in Bronze Age graves, it has been possible to reconstruct what was fashionable in the Middle Bronze Age.

In 2005 a discovery of a shipwreck off the coast of Salcombe in Devon shed new light on Britain's overseas ancient trade. Whilst the ship itself had rotted, gold and bronze jewellery was discovered in excellent condition.

Bronze Age Jewellery

Gemstones such as Jet and Amber were frequently used in Bronze Age jewellery.

DID YOU KNOW?

A primitive method for cutting and fashioning gemstones where one gemstone is hit or rubbed against another. Before the modern lap was invented most gemstones were shaped this way.

BRUTING

Burma
The most famous source of ruby on the planet.

Due to Burma's recent political instability and trade embargoes placed on the country, some of the world's finest Sapphires, Rubies and Spinels are not available in some countries such as America.

Although some gems have funded conflict (especially Jade which has been mined under military rule and therefore Burmese Jade should be totally avoided), many of the gems being smuggled out of the country along its border with Thailand are by small artisanal miners, who are selling the gems to support their families during the country's instability. The world's finest Rubies come from Burma and with all the country's recent traumas, with military rule and cyclones, if you can be sure of how the gems were mined and can trust your sources, and you can be sure some of your cash ends up directly in the pocket of those that need it most, then it surely adds even more beauty to the gems you acquire.

Although there are several areas in Burma where gems are unearthed, the most famous gem region in the country and possibly in the entire world is the Mogok Valley.

Known by many in the trade as the "Valley of

Rubies", it is without doubt the most important source of Rubies in the world.

The valley stretches for some twenty miles and at its widest point it exceeds two miles. The Rubies from this area are world renowned for their truly deep, intense red colour. They lack the presence of iron found in Rubies from other locations and this leads to a stronger fluorescence and an extremely vivid saturation.

The next most significant source of fine Rubies in Burma is Mong Hsu; this region lies between the Mogok Valley and the border with Thailand. Rubies discovered here tend to feature a hue that is a purplish red.

Although not as famous as its Rubies, Burma is also the source of some of the world's finest Sapphires, although unfortunately supply is incredibly limited. These tend to be of a very dark, intense, pure colour and are often referred to as "Royal Blue". They normally have a hue of around 80 to 85% blue, with the remainder being made up of purple. Compared to Kashmir (the other benchmark for Sapphires), Burmese Sapphires have better transparency. For me the perfect Sapphire would be one that has the openness of colour of a Kashmir, combined with the diaphaneity of a Burmese Sapphire.

Similar to most gem mining communities, there is very little technology or mechanisation involved in the industry, with most of the mining taking place in alluvial deposits, using buckets, spades and sieves.

Jaipurium

Used mainly for gemstones that are translucent to opaque, the cabochon cut is a dome shape with no facets other than its flat bottom.

Cabochon Cut

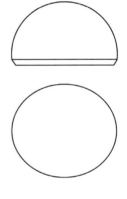

Normally the dome is highly polished to increase its lustre, and when viewed from above the outline of the cut is typically an oval. That said, round cut cabochons have become increasingly popular over the past four or five years.

Cutting "en cabochon" is also applied to gemstones which demonstrate optical phenomena such as asterism and chatoyancy.

The cabochon cut has been popular for over 2000 years. One word

of caution though: don't be tempted to polish the flat surface underneath a cabochon cut gem; it is intentionally left unpolished as it returns more light into the gem. If polished, you may find your gem is not as vivid in colour as before.

Cambodia

*Gems TV Presenter
Matt MacNamara
gem hunting in
Cambodia*

There are two main provinces in Cambodia that mine gemstones: Paillin in West Cambodia, near the Thai border and Ratanakiri in North East Cambodia, near the Vietnam border.

Paillin for many years has been the source of quality Sapphires. However, similar to its neighbours, yields over recent years have continued to fall and most mining in the region today is undertaken by small mining organisations.

The historic location of Ratanakiri is without any major roads and is virtually inaccessible (especially in the rainy season) by the outside world. The region is one of the most beautiful and undeveloped areas in Cambodia, where electricity and running water are almost non-existent. It is also one of the few places on Earth where traditional tribes still exist, cut off from the outside world.

Although their numbers are decreasing, it is estimated that some 60,000 tribespeople still reside in its tree-topped hills. Other than subsistence farming, gemstone mining is one of the few commercial activities to take place in the region. Ratanakiri actually derives its name from combining the Cambodian words for "gems" and "mountains".

Our camera man Derek filming artisanal miners in the hillside at Ratanakiri

The main gem mined in Ratanakiri is Zircon and many agree that some of the best quality in the world comes from this tribal area. Other mines produce limited quantities of Amethyst and Peridot.

There have also been several reports on the internet of Zircon being mined at Preah Vihear, very near to Angkor Wat (one of the seven wonders of the world). However, I have some very good friends who recently visited the area looking for this new source of Zircon and they came back empty handed, convinced that the only mining in the area is small families panning for gold. So do be careful when using the internet for research as you to could end up on a unfruitful journey.

Erecting a sun canopy to protect the local miners

Cameo

Sculptures or coins which use raised images are known as "cameos". One of the main gems used to create a cameo is Agate.

Several Agates are naturally discovered where the stone is made up of several distinct coloured layers. To imagine this, think of a white slice of bread sitting on top of a brown slice. The artist carves away at the white piece of bread and leaves a design where the raised image is white on a brown background, thus creating a cameo.

Some of the most impressive examples of cameos date as far back as the 6th century BC, found in amazing sculptures in Greece. Designs are normally portraits of famous people, biblical scenes or religious figures. While Agates are the most common gemstone used to make Cameos, shells and imitation gems are now also frequently used.

Unfortunately today, many cameo's are created where an object is sometimes carved by laser and then glued or welded onto a background with a contrasting colour. Obviously this is much cheaper than someone spending many hours hand carving the piece out of a single gemstone, where the piece chosen had a natural split of two colours. If you are spending a lot of money on a cameo, make sure that you pay attention with your loupe to where the two layers join.

Campbell and his famous tree-house

(Photos courtesy of Bruce Bridges)

In 1967, Scottish gemmologist Campbell R Bridges discovered a beautiful green gemstone hidden in a potato shaped rock in Tanzania.

After performing gemmological tests, he declared it Grossularite: an extremely rare member of the Garnet family. Unfortunately, very shortly after discovering the gem, the Tanzanian Government nationalised all mines and Campbell was forced to leave the country.

Not a man known to give up - and with Tiffany & Co. having already shown interest in the gem - Campbell traced the vein in which it was originally found back to Kenya. In 1971, after searching for the gem for over a year, he rediscovered it in the Tsavo National Park.

In order to protect his find, Campbell resided in treetops, using a pet python to guard the gems. Campbell was finally able to officially register the deposit and obtained permission to mine. In 1974, Campbell agreed with the then President of Tiffany & Co., Henry Platt, that the gem should be named after the park in which it was found, the name Tsavorite was agreed.

Tragically Campbell was murdered aged 71 on 11th August 2009 by a group of men due to a dispute over mining near the town of Voi, Kenya.

Campbell R Bridges
The famous gem hunter who discovered Tsavorite.

Campbell and Henry naming Tsavorite

Canada

The world's second largest country and now a major player in the Diamond market.

Canada is rapidly becoming a major player in the world of gemstone supply. Until 20 years ago, you would hardly have ever seen the country mentioned in gemstone books or being discussed by gem collectors. So what is all the fuss about? Diamonds.

Considering commercial Diamond mining only began in the 1990s, Canada became the world's third largest producer of Diamonds by 2003 and, according to data from the United States Geological Survey (USGS) in 2009, unearthed 12 million carats of gem quality Diamonds. Since the first mines opened in 1991 in the Lac de Gras area of the Northwest Territories, there has been a flurry of activity with new mines opening on a regular basis. So much so that experts predict that Canada will prove to be the largest source of Diamonds within the next few years.

But Canada is more than just a Diamond producer: Ammolite is found in Alberta; Emerald and Aquamarines are found in Yukon; and Amethyst mines can be found in Ontario. The country's other mining activities are very diverse. The largest export by carat weight is Nephrite Jade, mined in northern British Columbia, along with the blues of Sapphire and Iolite. A small amount of Opal is also exported.

As different gems have different densities, carat weights only have a loose bearing on the overall size of a gem.

The word originated from the Carob seed, which was once regarded as one of the most uniformed, naturally occurring items to be found on Earth, with each seed being similar in weight.

There are 5 carats to a gram and this measurement is now recognised around the world (even in the U.S. where the metric system isn't used). In 1907, a carat became recognised as the international measurement for gemstones when it was adopted by the General Conference on Weights and Measures (an international body set up in 1875 to set measurement standards). Prior to this, many countries in Europe, Persia and the Middle East all had their own measurements for weighing gemstones: whilst they all seem to have been linked to the carob seed, they all varied slightly. If you have inherited a gemstone ring that is over 100 years old, there is every chance that the weight detailed on the certificate (jewellery certificates were even more prevalent in previous centuries) is incorrect.

Carat
A measurement of weight that should only be applied to genuine gemstones.

Carbuncle
An ancient word used to describe red gemstones.

This is not a word you are going to come across too often in the modern gem world, but a short explanation may help when reading older literature, where it is frequently used.

Throughout the past 5000 years, names of gemstones have continually evolved, as better identification has led to a far wider array of different species. It is believed that the initial use of the word Carbuncle was to describe any gemstone that was red.

Over time, the word was further restricted to cabochon cut red gems and later in history it was adopted as the initial name for Ruby. At this time other civilisations were naming Ruby "ratnari", which is Sanskrit for "king of gems".

Carbuncles are mentioned in the Bible in Exodus 28:17 and 39:10; Ezekiel 28:13 (which refers to the Carbuncle's presence in the Garden of Eden) and Isaiah 54:12: "And I will make thy windows of agates, and thy gates of carbuncles, and all thy borders of pleasant stones."

It is quite fortunate that the name is no longer used as it is also, according to the dictionary, the name of a painful circumscribed inflammation, with a tendency to spread somewhat like a boil!

a rubber mould of the design. When this is completed, you will have an inverse of the original design into which liquid wax is injected. Once the wax has cooled you then remove it from the rubber mould and repeat the injection process as many times as the number of pieces of jewellery you wish to make.

Once completed, a jeweller checks each piece and corrects any imperfections by adding, removing or remodelling the waxes. Next all of the waxes are attached to what is known as a "wax tree".

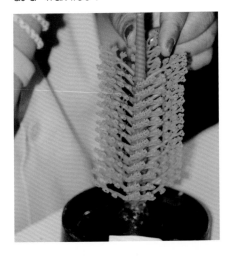

After the tree is assembled it is placed inside a cylinder into which an investment (casting material) is poured. If you ever made plaster of Paris models as a child, this is a similar technique, however the investment is an incredibly fine powder. We have used hundreds of different investments over the years, but right now the powder that provides the smooth finish on our gold and silver designs is actually mined in Derbyshire and is then flown to our facilities in India. Once the investment hardens, it is then placed in an oven at a temperature of between 800 to 1100 degrees Fahrenheit, at which the wax melts and is allowed to run out of the bottom of the cylinder.

Now you are left with a cast where there is an empty space for each ring. Next the gold or silver is poured into the top of the flask and it flows into all of the space that was previously occupied by the wax. The machinery in which this takes place is becoming more and more advanced. Some use centrifugal force to ensure the metal flows evenly into every small detail (imagine even the tiny prongs need to be made), others create a vacuum and some even do both. The more advanced the machine, the better the finish of the jewellery, the better the porosity of the metal, and the more accurate the piece will be.

Once the metal is cooled, the flask is quenched and the investment removed. Next the silversmith or goldsmith detaches the jewellery from what is now a metal tree and starts to file and polish the jewellery. The remaining tree stump, which is either solid gold or silver, is then refined and used once again. When completely polished, the jewellery is ready to be handed to the gemstone setter to add the final gemstones.

As you can see, the lost wax injection method is very complex, with many steps involved. At every stage skilled operators and jewellers are required. The quality of equipment used, the brand of wax, the type of injection machine, the grade of investment powders, the type of ovens, the sophistication of the casting machine: all of these have a direct effect on the quality of jewellery produced. Whilst all of the highest-grade of equipment and consumables are very expensive, in the long run a jeweller who invests in the best should always see a good return on their outlay through the quality of the jewellery they create.

One interesting point is that this casting method still needs a lot of work to be completed by competent jewellers. It's a jeweller who checks each piece of wax and improves the finish of it before it is assembled on to the wax tree. It is a jeweller who files, polishes and amends each piece after casting. It's a jeweller who sets each gemstone in the final stages and of course it is a highly skilled lapidarist who cuts, facets and polishes the gemstones in the first place. I tend to refer to jewellery that is cast not as 'hand made', as this would suggest no machinery was used at all, but as "hand crafted".

With the exception of "one of a kind" pieces, most rings, pendants and earrings are made this way today. Whilst the casting method is very efficient and flexible, it can obviously only cast one type of metal at a time. Therefore, when two metals are combined to make the same design, they are cast separately and then bonded together by the jeweller.

DID YOU KNOW?

A cavity is a gap in a rock, a hollow in limestone or cavernous lava. Tanzanite forms in large cavities, whilst Emeralds tend to be squeezed and compressed whilst creating their own cavity.

CAVITY

Previously known as Ceylon, the island of Sri Lanka, located south of India, has rightly earned its name as the 'Gem Island' (Ratna Dweepa). In addition to mining world-class Corundum (the family name for Rubies and Sapphires), the island is also home to Alexandrite, Garnet, Moonstone, Peridot, Spinel, Topaz, Tourmaline and Zircon.

Ceylon (Sri Lanka)

With the country's political situation now stabilised, international gem hunters are once again returning to this gem rich island

This island has been known for its splendid array of colourful Sapphires and deep red Rubies for over 2000 years. When it comes to Sapphire, Sri Lanka is best known for its Blue Sapphire (known as Ceylon Sapphire) and its stunning orangey pinkish Padparadscha Sapphire (named after the lotus flower also found on the island).

Ceylon Sapphire is typically a stunning light-blue gem with amazing clarity and it is possibly for this reason why Princess Diana chose an engagement ring featuring a Ceylon Sapphire as the central gem. The main source for the gem is the mining region of Ratnapura, located 65 miles southeast of Colombo, the capital of Sri Lanka. The town is also the main focal point for trading gems in Sri Lanka and its name in Singhalese means "gem city".

Mining in Sri Lanka is primarily undertaken by artisan miners (informal mining), however the government is working hard at putting more formal procedures in place, apparently for a twofold purpose: to help preserve the landscape and to increase the percentage of profit received by the miners for each and every gem found. In order to do this, they aim to increase the skill levels of gemstone cutters and gem treatment companies within the country.

The mines are generally based in alluvial deposits and old riverbeds. As in Madagascar, to access the layers of gem bearing deposits, the miners dig, by hand, small vertical holes 10 to 30 feet into the ground and then create tunnels horizontally. This avoids upsetting the landscape and is often less labour intensive than creating an open pit mine.

Often you will hear stories about the misidentification of gemstones. Ceylon with its treasure trove of different gemstones has played a lead role in many famous misidentifications. This could be because mining is primarily from small independent miners, most of whom don't have access to gem experts. Take Tourmaline for example: it was only identified as a separate gem species when a bag of "mixed gems" were sent from Ceylon to Holland in 1703. Then there was a parcel of gems sent to Dublin in the 1940s that was thought to be Spinel: one of the pieces turned out to be a new discovery, which we now know as Taaffeite.

Then there is the intentional misidentification. Some unscrupulous gem dealers to increase their profits, will name their Sapphires "Ceylon Sapphire" even if they have come from a different location.

Ceylon

● Columbo

● Ratnapura

Either used to display pendants and charms or as a piece of jewellery in its own right, the chain has been used for many centuries. Although most metal chains (including gold and silver) are made by machine, there are a few artisan jewellers around the globe that still make every link by hand.

Chain

Worn on its own as a single piece of jewellery or as an accessory for displaying pendants.

There are numerous names for standard styles of chains and these include: bill chain; barrel and link chain; belcher chain; cord chain; curb chain; Diamond trace chain; rope chain; strap chain; trace chain. Many of these chains on sale in Europe are produced in Italy, Turkey and Germany.

Be extra careful of buying cheap chains abroad! My assistant Barry once bought a chain on a Spanish beach, after seeing it had an 18k stamp. When he brought it into the office the following week, I explained to him that it was not an official hallmark; it turned out to be polished brass! When it comes to gold if the price seems too good to be true it is probably not as described.

The first country to fully develop machine made chains was Italy; hot on their heels were engineers in Turkey and more recently a handful of German companies who employ some of the world's most technically admired technicians. Note my use of the words 'engineers' and 'technicians'. When it comes to machine made chains, the skill set required is very different to that of the silversmiths and goldsmiths who hand make chains in areas such as Bali and India.

To learn more about how chains are made via machinery and not hand, I visited one of my main chain suppliers in Germany to see how they do it. Their business started over 100 years ago when they made chains in a more similar fashion that I am used to seeing in our hand made jewellery facility in India. As you can imagine, being German they were always looking to develop new methods and machinery to make stronger and more cost effective chains. Marcus, who runs the company is its fourth generation, spent a whole day enthusiastically showing me the various different types of machines they use for making a wide array of styles.

Although there is a different machine for every different style of chain, they all follow the same principle. First, various metals are annealed together to make the correct alloy. When they have cooled they are in a form of a wire that is approximately 1cm in diameter. Next the wire is milled to take on a more narrow form. It is then once again heated, but not to melting point, just enough to make it more malleable. Next, it is reduced to the required gauge for the chain that is to be made. So now you have, for example, a long reel of say 50 metres

of 1mm gauge solid 925 Sterling Silver. Now depending on the style of chain, whether it be a belcher, an anchor cut, a twisted link, curb, trace chain etc, the reel is loaded onto a machine that has been specially designed to make that style and size of chain. The machines are typically four foot high and less than three foot square; surprisingly small for the job they do.

Once the machine starts running, it twists the wire, creates the link, cuts the wire, inserts the next link inside the first and starts to automatically assemble the chain. The type of chain being assembled affects the speed at which the machine operates at, however most machines can run at around one hundred links per minute.

Once the chain has been assembled it is still one very long length of around 20 or 30 metres, but at this stage it is still weak as the links are effectively just jump rings.

The next process is to cover the entire chain in a silver welding powder and put it through a very large machine. With the exception of where the joint is situated, it removes all of the power from the chain and then each link is heated, welded and connected together. Once completed the joints are even stronger than the actual links themselves and have as illness in the human body and is believed to happen when the body holds onto negative energy (through problems with rotation in certain Chakra). Having a finely tuned Chakra system means that negative energy is not trapped, thus allowing it to escape from the body easily.

Chakra can be healed and cleansed by gemstones, colour and sound. Concentrating on certain colours or sounds is believed to aid the overall balance of the Chakras. For example, the Throat Chakra is cleansed by the colour blue and the noise created from the word "eye". Try it yourself – imagine your throat, the colour blue and make the sound of the word "eye". Keep doing this for as long as you can.

Gemstones are believed to be in tune with Chakra by their colour and vibration. It is believed that applying a gemstone, usually directly onto the skin, can have a beneficial effect on the Chakra, Here is a list of the seven Chakra and their related gemstones…

1. Root Chakra
Garnet, Black Tourmaline, Haematite, Smokey Quartz, Bloodstone and Ruby.

Haematite

The Root Chakra is connected with our sense of earth and grounding. It is also beneficial to instinct and survival.
Location: Base of the spine (coccyx)
Colour: Blood-red (secondary color is black)

2. Sacral Chakra
Amber, Azurite, Malachite, Clear Quartz, Jade, Ruby, Carnelian and Citrine.

Malachite

Related to water, emotions and sexuality, it connects with our grace, depth of feeling and ability to accept change.
Location: Lower abdomen
Colour: Orange

3. Solar Plexus Chakra
Citrine, Amber, Moonstone, Peridot, Calcite and Topaz.

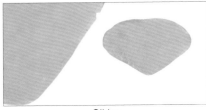
Citrine

Related to our willpower, creativity and autonomy, it brings us energy and spontaneity.

Location: Bellow the chest
Colour: Yellow

4. Heart Chakra
Malachite, Emerald, Green Tourmaline, Rose Quartz, Kunzite and Rhodochrosite.

Kunzite

The middle Chakra of the seven is the Heart Chakra, related to love, persona, mind and body; it helps us love, have peace and feel compassion.
Location: Center of the chest
Colour: Green (secondary color is pink)

5. Throat Chakra
Lapis Lazuli, Sapphire, Aquamarine, Turquoise, Kyanite, Blue Topaz and Azurite.

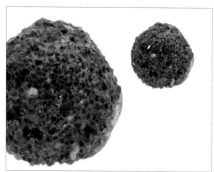
Azurite

This is located around the throat and therefore is related to communication and also creativeness.
Location: Throat area
Colour: Blue

6. Brow Chakra
Turquoise, Watermelon Tourmaline, Labradorite, Amethyst and Moonstone.

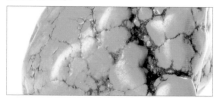
Turquoise

Also known as the 'Third Eye' Chakra, it is believed to relate to the act of seeing - both physically and intuitively. When this Chakra is healthy it gives clarity of thought and vision.
Location: Center of the forehead, between the eyebrows.
Colour: Blue through Indigo

7.Crown Chakra
Amethyst, Opal, Tourmaline, Diamond and Clear Quartz.

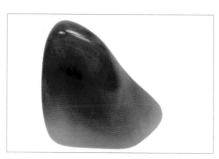
Amethyst

The Crown Chakra has a direct association with consciousness, to give knowledge and understanding in spiritual connections and bliss.
Location: Top of the head
Color: Purple

Numbers

As well as giving the appropriate numbered charm on the 16th, 18th and 21st birthday, individual numbers have specific meanings throughout history.

1. Symbolises God
2. Love and duality
3. The three virtues of faith, hope and charity
4. Balance and organisation
5. Harmony and divine grace
6. Longevity but unfortunately also the number associated with evil
7. A lucky number in many cultures
8. Perfection, prosperity and infinity
9. Achievement and patience

Pig

The pig is making a big comeback in the charm world. The animal has grown to represent sincerity, honesty, intelligence and kindness.

Scarab (beetle)

An ancient Egyptian symbol to represent the circle of life from creation to resurrection.

Shells

Worn as charms for thousands of years, the shell today symbolises romance and femininity.

Stars

Worn as a talisman for thousands of years, the star is said to protect the wearer as well as to provide guidance.

Sun

The sun represents power, warmth, eternity and hope.

Charoite

A lavender to purple gemstone, sometimes wrongly named as "purple Turquoise."

When the gem was first discovered in Siberia, Russia in the 1940s, it was simply known as the "Lilac Stone". In the 1970s the gem burst onto the international gem scene and it was renamed Charoite after the river Charo from where it is mined. To-date this remains the only known location for this gemstone.

Its appearance is similar to how you might imagine a purple Turquoise to look, with individual swirling patterns of white, grey and black veins and a lustre that appears slightly silky. Its structure can be compared to a Lapis Lazuli as it too is constructed of several minerals including Feldspar and Tinaksite (a complex mineral composed of many elements including Calcium, Manganese, Titanium and Iron).

Similar to Turquoise, the gemstone is normally reconstituted to make it more durable for setting in jewellery. For this reason, as is the case with Turquoise, cleaning your jewellery with a steam or ultrasonic cleaner is not recommended.

Crystal Healers believe that Charoite jewellery should be placed beneath your pillow to aid a good night's sleep and that the gem helps to cleanse and purify the body.

Colour	Lavander, Purple
Hardness	5.6
SG	2.54 -2.78
RI	1.50 - 159
Crystal	Monoclinic
Composition	K(Ca,Na)$_2$ Si$_4$O$_1$)

The word chatoyancy is used to describe an optical effect that certain gems have, which resemble the opening and closing of eyes.

The phenomenon is commonly called cat's eye effect, for when the light hits the surface of the polished gemstone, a narrow line of light appears, which looks dramatically similar to that of a cat's eye. Chatoyancy is an effect caused by tiny fibrous inclusions that are naturally arranged in a parallel configuration.

For a gemstone to show this effect it must be cabochon cut, and its inclusions must run parallel to the base. Examples of gems that can feature chatoyancy are: Tourmaline, Sapphire, Quartz, Chrysoberyl, Fibrolite and of course, Tiger's Eye.

One word of warning: I spoke to a lady once who told me that her beloved Chrysoberyl had lost its cat's eye look. After asking her for more detail, she informed me that a few days prior it had been cleaned by a friend. What transpired was that the friend had not only cleaned the top of the cabochon cut gem, but also polished the flat surface underneath. The result was that light which was previously locked in the gem, now seeped through the bottom.

Chatoyancy
From the French words "chat oeil," meaning cat's eye.

Checkerboard Cut

Add a little scintillation into your life.

A style of faceting the table and crown of gemstones that often increases the surface scintillation of the gem. The best way to imagine this style of cutting is to visualise a chessboard rotated so one of the corners is resting on a desk and the individual black and white shapes are no longer square, but Diamond-like in appearance.

The cut is normally applied to large coloured gemstones and is particularly popular on cushion shaped gems. Although the effect usually covers the entire gem above the girdle, it is occasionally only applied to the crown.

It is normally applied to opaque and translucent gems, although occasionally it is used for transparent gems that are lighter in tone. As mentioned above, the style lends itself to cushion shaped gems; however it can also add an extra dimension to trilliant, oval and heart shapes. A well-cut checkerboard, will display incredible surface lustre. Rock it backwards and forwards slightly and you should see facets light up and off similar to lights on a Christmas tree (this is effect is known as scintillation). In China, where gems are often cut by machines, the checkerboard cut is now featuring more often.

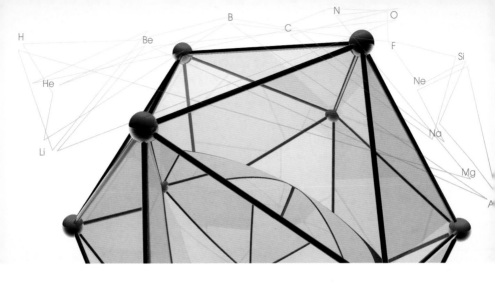

For most gemstones in this book we detail the chemical composition on the bottom of each chart. But what do all of those little symbols mean and why do we need to understand anything about them? Having a basic understanding of elements will help you in understanding how some gems are different to others and how many of them receive their fabulous colours.

So let's start really basic. Everything you can touch is made up of elements. Your body, a gemstone, flowers, a car, this book, a table: all are made of elements. Even gas and air are made of elements. Our bodies, for example, are made of mostly oxygen, with a fair amount of carbon added to the mix.

Elements, as in the periodic table, are either pure (as in a Diamond which is pure Carbon - the periodic symbol being "C"), or like our bodies a chemical compound; a mixture of two or more elements. There are only 118 elements so far discovered by man and therefore everything you see on earth is made from very similar elements, but just mixed into different cocktails.

There are some pure elements that you can't see such as hydrogen and helium, and then others that you can such

Chemical Elements

The chemical make up of our body is not dissimilar to that of a diamond.

as Silver, Gold, Copper, Titanium, Iron, Nickel, Palladium, and Rhodium.

But what is an element? Well, this book is not about electrochemistry and you really don't need to be a chemist to get the best out of your gemstones, so let's try and summarise this in as few words as possible. An element is a substance that is made purely from one type of atom. An atom is the absolute smallest possible amount of a chemical element you could have, therefore an atom of silver is the smallest amount of silver possible. How big is the average atom? About

positively charged proton, Helium is second in the periodic table because its nuclei has two positively charged protons, Lithium has three protons, Beryllium has four, Boron five, Carbon six, and so on. Around the outside of the nuclei are electrons which orbit the nuclei. Imagine the nuclei to be our planet, with hundreds of satellites orbiting around it at break neck speed and you kind of understand the principles of how atoms are structured. To make things simple for us, the number of electrons (the satellites) are always equal to the number of protons (positively charged particles).

Let's compare two different elements. If you could split open a Gold atom, you would find 79 positively charged protons and 118 uncharged neutrons in its centre (nuclei), around which you would find 79 high speed electrons orbiting its perimeter. Whereas another metal more commonly found on Earth Iron, has just 26 protons and 30 neutrons, being orbited by 26 electrons.

100,000 times thinner than the width of a piece of human hair! Atoms vary from one another based on how the centre of the atom (the nuclei or nucleus) is composed. This centre is composed of protons and neutrons. Protons are simply positively charged particles, and neutrons are uncharged particles. The number of protons in an atom dictates its atomic number. Hydrogen is the first element in the periodic table because it only has one

You can find out the atomic mass (atomic weight), by adding the number of neutrons and the number of protons together. Helium for example has a

relative atomic mass of four (it has two protons and two neutrons) whereas Gold as we can see above has 79 protons and 118 neutrons making its atomic mass 197. Haven't we learnt a lot in just two pages? We now know how to weigh atoms!

Let's briefly explain molecules and compounds. A molecule is two or more atoms that have joined together. They could be two atoms that are the same or two atoms that are different. Compound elements are formed when two or more different types of atoms join together. A gold bar will have lots of gold atoms joined together, lots of molecules, but it is not a compound because all the molecules are gold. Whereas water is made by two atoms of hydrogen linking up with a single atom of oxygen (H_2O): this is therefore a compound. But it's also a molecule because there is more than one atom.

Let's not go as far as splitting the atom, because that's way too complex and of no use to us in gemmology. My friend gives an analogy that makes it easy to comprehend elements, atoms, molecules and compounds. You are in an ice cream shop and in the fridge there are 118 different flavours of ice cream, these are your elements to put into your big ice cream cone. One scoop of any of these flavours is your atom. If I want two or more scoops we are going to call my ice cream a molecule. If I want to have one part strawberry and one part chocolate, then it becomes a compound. An element is a basic substance that can't be simplified (hydrogen, gold, silver etc). An atom is the smallest amount of an element (single scoop of ice cream). A molecule is two or more atoms that are chemically joined together (H_2, O_2, H_2O etc). A compound is a molecule that contains more than one different element (Al_2O_3 – the chemical compound for Sapphire, etc).

On the following page we have listed elements in order of their Atomic number, along with their symbol and Atomic weight.

The gemstone with the simplest chemical formula is of course Diamond which is pure carbon. No other gemstone is made from just one element. Quartz such as Amethyst and Citrine also has a fairly simple formula SiO_2 (Silicon Dioxide). Amethyst then has a trace of iron impurities which provide the gem with its infamous colour, however small amounts of trace elements are rarely written in the formula of a gemstone. If they were, for Amethyst, which has approximately 30 to 40 parts per million, you would see $Fe4+$ added to the end of the formula.

Other gemstones such as Garnets have a more complicated formula and Topaz which is comprised of aluminium, silicon, hydrogen, oxygen and fluorine looks like $Al_2SiO_4(F,OH)_2$ when written down. However, the winner in terms of complicated chemical formulae, a gemstone that is a true cocktail of elements is Tourmaline - $(Na,Ca)(Mg,Li,Al,Fe2+)_3Al_6(BO_3)_3Si_6O_{18}(OH)_4$.

Atomic Number	Element	Symbol	Atomic Weight
1	Hydrogen	H	1
2	Helium	He	4
3	Lithium	Li	7
4	Beryllium	Be	9
5	Boron	B	11
6	Carbon	C	12
7	Nitrogen	N	14
8	Oxygen	O	16
9	Fluorine	F	19
10	Neon	Ne	20
11	Sodium	Na	23
12	Magnesium	Mg	24
13	Aluminum	Al	27
14	Silicon	Si	28
15	Phosphorus	P	31
16	Sulfur	S	32
17	Chlorine	Cl	35
18	Argon	Ar	40
19	Potassium	K	39
20	Calcium	Ca	40
22	Titanium	Ti	48
23	Vanadium	V	51
24	Chromium	Cr	52
25	Manganese	Mn	55

In Europe, chokers tend to be 14" to 15" in length, where as necklaces are normally 16" to 20" in length. Worn by royalty and the rich and famous, chokers are often seen as an essential piece of jewellery for those attending prestigious events.

Whereas most necklaces are made out of precious metals, chokers often tend to be made out of softer materials, so that they sit more comfortably on the neck. Velvet, lace, leather and ribbons are used to support gemstones and they are normally connected to the choker with a fastening that can easily be detached.

Elizabeth Taylor often wore chokers and today many brides wear Pearl chokers on their big day. This trend of wedding chokers seems to have started not in Europe but in Hollywood, where often the choker (normally made of Pearls and silver) becomes the focal point of the entire outfit, with the dress being styled around it.

Another style of choker is the "gothic choker", these rarely have gemstones set into them and tend to be made of dark coloured materials such as black lace or velvet rather than metals.

Choker

A style of necklace that sits high around the neck.

Christian Names and Gemstones

There has been a tradition that dates back many centuries where certain gemstones are associated with Christian names. Possibly the most famous gemmologist of the last two 200 years, George F. Kunz, wrote in his book "The Curious Lore of Precious Stones", "...there is established a very pretty custom of assigning to the various masculine and feminine Christian names a particular gem". It is believed by many to be a very strong talisman when the correct Christian name gem is worn and the effect is believed to be even stronger when the gem is set alongside one's birthstone.

For thousands of years man has worn gems to bring about good luck, fortune and to promote good health. On the whole, as the world becomes more connected and more educated our belief in anything we cannot touch or feel diminishes. So why do so many people still wear gemstones for their crystal healing and talisman powers? I believe, that like me, many people feel the positive effects from gems, as a direct result of the belief itself. Effectively the gemstones provide the catalyst for an effect known as placebo.

Most people are aware of the GIA's (Gemological Institution of America) grading system for Diamonds, however few are aware of their clarity grading for coloured gems.

Clarity Grading for Coloured Gems

It is important to explain that Mother Nature's wide array of gemstones are formed by several different natural processes. While some are exposed to immense pressure, others are created at extreme temperatures and are then cooled rapidly, whilst other gem types develop in soluble liquids.

quality Emerald would only be comparable to a poor clarity Topaz.

Due to the different circumstances in which they are created, some gem varieties naturally have better clarity than others. For example, in terms of clarity, a top

For this reason, the GIA have devised a grading system that separates the main gem varieties into the three groups; Type I, Type II and Type III.

Type I gem varieties are those that form under conditions that normally result in gemstones that are eye clean.

Type II gemstones are those that more often have noticeable inclusions, but not always noticable with the naked eye.

The final grading, Type III, is reserved for gemstones that have had a very traumatic upbringing, with immense pressure and a violent gemmological home-life: these gems are only in the rarest of occasions eye clean and normally have very visible inclusions.

Put simplistically, knowing if the gem you are looking to buy is a Type I, Type II or Type III will help you in analysing whether its level of clarity is good for that gem type or not. To the right we have tried to simplify the GIA system for grading the clarity of coloured gemstones. Look for the subtle difference in wording between the three different types, in the higher ratings.

At Gems TV we use the GIA Coloured Gemstone Grading System for our gemstones. However, as we tend to sell multiples of the same gemstones rather than one piece at a time, we have to be a little bit more approximate in our grading to allow for small variances in one gemstone to another. Therefore we simplify our grading by reducing the seven grades to just four. Rather than having Si1 and Si2 for example (Si means slightly included), we just grade items Si.

This unheated Aquamarine is a type1 gemstone.

Sapphire is a type 2 gemstone

Rubillite is a type 3 gemstone

	Type I	Type II	Type III
Gems	Aquamarine, Morganite, Chrysoberyl, Smokey Quartz, Kunzite, Topaz, Green Tourmaline, Blue Zircon, Tanzanite.	Alexandrite, Sapphire, Ruby, Garnet, Iolite, Peridot, Amethyst, Citrine, Spinel, Tourmaline, Zircon.	Emerald, Red Tourmaline (Rubellite), Pink Tourmaline, Watermelon Tourmaline
VVS	Very, Very Slightly Included - Minute inclusions that are difficult to see using 10X, and are not visible at all to the naked eye	Very, Very Slightly Included – Minor inclusions that are somewhat easy to see using 10X, but still not visible to the naked eye	Very, Very Slightly Included – Noticeable inclusions that are easy to see using 10X, but usually not visible to the naked eye
VS	Very Slightly Included – Minor inclusions that are easier to see using 10X, but still not visible to the naked eye	Very Slightly Included - Noticeable inclusions that are easier to see using 10X, and may be slightly visible to the naked eye	Very Slightly Included - Obvious inclusions that are easy to see using 10X, and usually visible to the naked eye.
SI1	Slightly Included 1 – The inclusions are easily seen using 10X, and are noticeable with the naked eye	Slightly Included 1 – The inclusions are easily seen using 10X and are large or numerous, and are noticeable with the naked eye.	Slightly Included 1 – The inclusions are large and numerous using 10X, and prominent with the naked eye.
SI2	Slightly Included 2 – The inclusions are more easily seen using 10X, and are quite visible with the naked eye	Slightly Included 2 – The inclusions are easily seen using 10X and are large or numerous, and are very noticeable with the naked eye	Slightly Included 2 – The inclusions are large and numerous using 10X, and very prominent with the naked eye
I1	Included 1 - The inclusions are very obvious and they have a moderate negative effect on the overall appearance or durability of the gemstone	Included 1 – The inclusions are very obvious and they have a moderate negative effect on the overall appearance or durability of the gemstone	Included 1 – The inclusions are very obvious and they have a moderate negative effect on the overall appearance or durability of the gemstone
I2	Included 2 - The inclusions are very obvious and they have a severe negative effect on the overall appearance or durability of the gemstone	Included 2 – The inclusions are very obvious and they have a severe negative effect on the overall appearance or durability of the gemstone	Included 2 – The inclusions are very obvious and they have a severe negative effect on the overall appearance or durability of the gemstone
I3	Included 3 – The inclusions are very obvious and they have a severe negative effect on both the overall appearance and durability of the gemstone	Included 3 – The inclusions are very obvious and they have a severe negative effect on both the overall appearance and durability of the gemstone	Included 3 – The inclusions are very obvious and they have a severe negative effect on both the overall appearance and durability of the gemstone

Clarity of Diamonds

Although not the most important criteria when selecting a Diamond, it is still one worth understanding before making an investment.

Few things in nature are perfect: this includes Diamonds. As with other gemstones, Diamonds have internal features, which are called inclusions and can sometimes have surface imperfections, which are known as blemishes or flaws.

The level of these inclusions and blemishes set the Diamond's level of clarity. This level, along with its colour, quality of cut and carat weight, will have a direct impact on both the Diamond's rarity and its price. Though clarity characteristics may have a negative effect on a Diamond's value, they are incredibly useful to separate a Diamond from its fake competitors, whose man-made inclusions, if present, are noticeably different to those of the real thing.

As no two Diamonds have the same inclusions or characteristics, it is possible to identify individual Diamonds from their inclusion fingerprint. Inclusions have also helped scientists identify how Diamonds are formed.

Blemishes do not necessarily have an overall impact on value, as any surface scratches or imperfections can be removed. This is not true of inclusions. If they are close to the surface they can of course be removed by re-cutting the gem; however, this obviously impacts on the overall Diamond weight.

Combined with the other three Cs (colour, cut and carat weight), a Diamond's clarity has a direct influence on its value: the cleaner the gem, the rarer it becomes. Flawless is the top grade in the Gemological Institute of America's (GIA) clarity grading system. Diamonds graded Flawless have no visible inclusions or blemishes under 10x magnification. Flawless Diamonds are extremely rare; to put it into context, it is possible to spend a lifetime in the industry without ever seeing one.

Although there are other standards used in the jewellery industry, the most widely used clarity guide is that of the GIA. This scale is intended to be used for Diamonds over a fifth of a carat.

Flawless (FL)
A flawless Diamond shows no inclusions or blemishes under 10x magnification.

Internally Flawless (IF)
To classify as an IF, a Diamond must show no inclusions under 10x magnification but can have some minor blemishes such as surface grain lines. Sometimes these blemishes can be removed by a lapidarist and polished to become a Flawless Diamond.

Very Very Slightly Included
(VVS1 and VVS2)
These Diamonds contain extremely tiny inclusions that are difficult to see or identify under 10x magnification. Usually the inclusions appear like pinpoints, tiny feathers, internal graining or tiny cavities.

Very Slightly Included
(VS1 and VS2)
These Diamonds contain small or minor inclusions that can be observed under 10x magnification by experienced jewellers (unless trained in Diamond grading you would be unlikely to spot them under this magnification). Normally VS Diamonds have small included crystals, small clouds or small feathers.

Slightly Included
(SI1 and SI2)
Slightly included Diamonds contain inclusions noticeable under 10x magnification to a jeweller. Typically, these inclusions are clouds, included crystals, knots, cavities or feathers. In addition to the GIA system, many in the trade will talk about an SI3 grade as being somewhere between SI2 and I1. However, even though the European Gemmological Laboratory (EGL) now recognises the grading, to-date the GIA have not added it to their official guide.

Included
(I1, I2 and I3)
Included Diamonds are where inclusions are obvious under 10x magnification, they might contain large feathers, or large included crystals. Usually this kind of inclusion can affect transparency and brilliance.

Beyond I3 there are Diamonds that have inclusions visible to the naked eye: these are referred to as Pique or PK and some in the industry often talk about them as "frozen spit".

As a rule of thumb, if you are buying a Solitaire Diamond Ring you should try and purchase an I1 or above. If this is out of your budget, then often it is worth buying a smaller carat weight to achieve this quality.

For Trilogy Diamond Rings or Eternity Bands, try and stretch to I2 or better.

When it comes to buying a Cluster Diamond Ring or one with accented Diamonds, then choosing I3 or above will often be fine. Of course, that said, different people have different opinions.

If a retailer does not specify what quality the Diamonds are, then either they don't know - in which case it is questionable whether you should buy from them (after all, even the worst car salesman knows what power the engine is) - or, worse still, they don't want you to know!

(which were only first discovered in the 1980s), there has more recently been a small deposit discovered in northern Siberia. However, the gems from this region tend to be a far darker reddish brown and they are slightly softer on the mohs scale. From our extensive research into this gem, we believe that to-date there has been no more than a couple of thousand carats ever faceted!

In addition to the tiny pockets unearthed in Tajikistan and Siberia, there have also been small discoveries of Clinohumite in such countries as Tasmania, Austria, Brazil and Canada: however none of these have yet to yield any gem grade material.

When yellow, the hue is very pure, and when orange, its colour can be a blend of yellow, and light and dark orange. Its key colour (the colour of its brilliance) is always lighter than its body colour and as you rotate the gem back and forwards its pleochroism can be mesmerising. Some of the pieces we have set into jewellery recently have resembled the array of warm, glowing colours you will see in the bottom of a roaring fireplace. The gem is normally included, but due to its incredible rarity and breathtaking colour, its inclusions are easily forgiven.

In some pieces the inclusions are microscopic and run throughout the entire piece. When this is the case, the gem becomes translucent rather than transparent. Although these are slightly less expensive than transparent pieces, they are still highly collectable.

In terms of carat weights, most pieces that we have sourced are less than half a carat; however we recently sold one piece that was 8.2 carats.

Clinohumite is a fine example of how indigenous people from different regions around the world know the same gemstones by different names. Locals in the Pamir mountains say they have been collecting "The Mountain Fire" (Clinohumite) for thousands of years.

Gemologist Yuri Zhukov tells a story of how on a visit to Tajik Pamir he came across an elderly gentleman who claimed to be 114 years old. He offered to give away a 44 gram (220 carat) piece of Clinohumite as he wanted it to carry on bringing good luck to those who held it and that he didn't want to take this piece of the sun to his grave. The stone had been in his family for over 400 years, but he was convinced that on his death his children, against his wishes, would bury the gemstone alongside him.

DID YOU KNOW?

This is an effect often seen in gems such as Paraiba Tourmaline and Emeralds, which is normally caused by a mass of small inclusions, often of a fibrous nature.

CLOUDY

Cluster Rings
There's more lustre in a cluster.

Nothing catches the eye more than a flash of scintillation off the table or crown facets of a gemstone. Big solitaire rings are great for showing off gems with a vivid saturation, while trilogy rings are symbols of love. With their mass of facets scintillating like lights on a Christmas tree, cluster rings are real head turners. I have a saying: 'there is more lustre in a cluster', a term which many of the jewellery presenters I have trained over the years now use as often as 'trilogy rings represent the past, the present and the future'.

Whilst it is true that smaller gemstones normally cost less than larger ones, the extra cost involved in faceting lots of gemstones, then sorting them to find the very best matches in colour and clarity and then having the jeweller set each gem individually in the ring, cannot be underestimated. Some cluster rings produced by Tomas Rae for example, have taken two days just to set the gems in each piece.

Although most cluster rings tend to have the same gemstones set, occasionally using different colours can often result in a stunning piece being created. Because gemstones vary in colour and clarity

Big, bold and colourful: the cocktail ring has long been a fabulous accessory for women all over the world.

Cocktail Rings
Providing the ultimate look in luxury jewellery.

Most cultures at some point or another have used jewellery for adornment, and in Western cultures extravagant jewellery has been enjoyed for many years. What better way to do this than with a cocktail ring? They really are show stoppers of incredible beauty and usually exquisitely designed.

Traditionally worn on the fourth finger on the right hand, from the Diamond trading slogans 'Your left hand says "we" and your right hand says "me"', and, 'Your left hand rocks the cradle and your right hand rocks the world', they are also known as right hand rings and Dinner Rings.

Cocktail rings gained popularity in the 1920s at the start of the Art Deco period, when dazzling jewellery was produced in stark contrast to other periods. The fashion for women was to have short hair, and they wore clothes such as flapper dresses. The jewellery fashion of this period was alluring and luxurious. It was the done thing to listen to jazz and be a free spirit, and the flamboyant jewellery complemented the playful and decadent attitude of the time. In

America, where illegal cocktail parties were held during the prohibition period (1920 – 1933), it was thought of as daring and controversial to be seen at the parties wearing these bright dazzling cocktail rings. Women would show their defiance of the law and flaunt their wealth and style at these soirees.

They can be absolutely breathtaking and allow the wearer to step into a world of high-class glamour and delight. They are unquestionably stylish, stunning and sexy; ostentatious yet graceful. A cocktail ring generally has one exciting gemstone that is the main focus of the ring, although it may have other gemstones that will complement it, while not distracting from the focal piece. They can also feature pearls, especially black pearls, as well as cabochon cut gemstones.

A cocktail ring gemstone normally starts at around 3 carats in size. Cocktail rings are an excellent way to spice up any outfit. Today, celebrities are often seen at film premieres and openings wearing cocktail rings. Whether it be Sarah Jessica Parker from "Sex and the City", who wore a huge, knuckle-sized cocktail ring for the final episode party of the

show or Angelina Jolie who has worn huge Emerald cocktail rings in the past, the stars of today seem to have the same love affair with these rings as their predecessors, inspiring a whole new generation to start wearing them. From Madonna to royalty, it seems the cocktail ring is enjoyed and celebrated by all.

Boodles, Graff, Chopard, Lorique and Bulgari are all making exquisite pieces, often in restricted numbers. Mixing old school glamour with witty design is one of the best ways of wearing the cocktail ring. Coco Channel herself, with her renowned avant-garde taste, was often seen wearing cocktail rings.

High Pressure
High Temperature (HPHT)

Effectively this treatment recreates the same environment in which the Diamond was formed 90 miles below the Earth's surface several billions of years ago. This technique is sometimes used on some White Diamonds simply to improve their appearance and in others where there are impurities of nitrogen trapped within the gem, it turns them a wonderful yellow to yellowish green colour.

Irradiation

This is the most common form of treatment for coloured Diamonds and it is similar to the process that has been used to turn seemingly colourless Topaz into wonderful Swiss and London blues. A similar treatment was first discovered in 1904 when Sir William Crookes, who was a chemist by trade and gemstone collector by night, discovered that you could change the colour of a Diamond by using radiation.

How does it work? Well, whereas natural coloured Diamonds receive their colour from impurities, irradiation promotes changes in the gem's atomic structure.

There are four slightly different processes currently used by the gemstone industry to irradiate Diamonds: all are safe and the majority of irradiated Diamonds on the market today have been treated in very expensive laboratories in New York. The colours from the irradiation process tend to be very dark and in fact nearly all Black Diamonds are treated by irradiation and heat. In1950, scientists realised that after the irradiation process had been completed, if you then heat treated (known as the 'annealing' process) the gemstone, beautiful, lighter shades could be formed. The overwhelming majority of Blue, Red, Green and Orange Diamonds on the market today have undergone this dual process.

One thing my good friend Rahul tells me (he owns Lotus Colors Inc; one of the largest coloured Diamond companies in the USA) is that when you put Diamonds through this process, as you are not introducing any other elements in the way you would with gemstone diffusion, you never know what colour the Diamonds will be at the end of the process!

Coated Diamonds

One of the few colours that cannot be created by HPHT or Irradiation is pure pink. Therefore a few years ago there was a vast amount of development undertaken by a few USA Diamond suppliers to create a coating that turns Diamonds pink.

Once they mastered the technique, as it is impossible to predict what colours will be produced from the irradiation process, in order to fulfil customer orders for specific hues and tones, they also started to coat Diamonds in other popular colours.

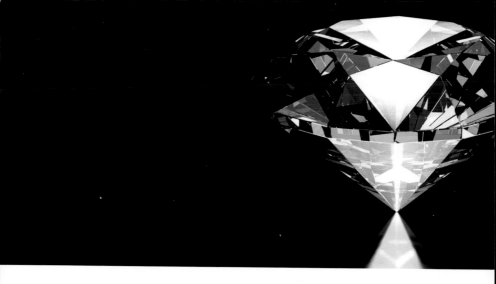

Colour Grading of Diamonds

Possibly the most important factor when selecting a Diamond.

Many people are under the assumption that Diamonds are always colourless, but this is in fact untrue. Diamonds actually come in a wide range of colours, such as the famous blue Hope Diamond, or the 128ct canary yellow Tiffany Diamond.

Whilst diamonds that have strong striking colours are amongst the most expensive items on the planet, when it comes to white diamonds it is those that are truly colourless that demand the higher prices.

The reason for this is that a truly colourless diamond allows light to travel though the gemstone better, therefore maximizing the gems wonderful brilliance and fire. Its like comparing clear glass to a lightly stained glass in a church window. The more colour in the glass, the less colours that can be seen through it. The more yellow a tint a Diamond has, the more it masks the gems ability to exhibit the colours of the rainbow.

Because Diamonds are not all the same colour, the Gemological Institute of America (GIA) introduced a Diamond Colour scale. This colour scale is the most widely used and was developed by Richard T. Liddicoat in the 1950s.

The scale is from D to Z: these letters do not represent or describe the actual colour of the Diamond, but instead represent how colourless the Diamond is. D is totally colourless while Z is pale yellow or brown. Obviously, the less colour the better it will display its unique fire and brilliance. Whilst the GIA scale is shown to the right, there are several other standards used by organisations such as AGS and CIBJO.

Whilst in the UK the GIA is the most well known scale for measuring g the colour grade of a Diamond, internationally there are several other standards. Just in case you are buying Diamonds abroad we have tried to make a chart that compares these different standards. Please note that this chart is an approximate representation of how the different organisations grade the colour of Diamonds. To put this together we first took the GIA scale and then matched as best as we could the scales from AGS (American Gem Society) and CIBJO (The World Jewellery Confederation) and the IDC (International Diamond Council).

GIA	Grade	GIA	CIBJO IDC
D	Colourless	0	Exceptional White +
E	Colourless	1	Exceptional White
F	Colourless	2	Rare White +
G	Colourless	3	Rare White
H	Near Colourless	4	White
I	Near Colourless	5	Slightly Tinted White
J	Near Colourless	6	Tinted White
K	Faint Yellow	7	
L	Faint Yellow	8	
M	Faint Yellow	9	
N	Very Light Yellow		
O	Very Light Yellow		
P	Very Light Yellow		
Q	Very Light Yellow		
R	Very Light Yellow		
S	Very Light Yellow		
T	Light Yellow	10	Tinted Colour
U	Light Yellow		
V	Light Yellow		
W	Light Yellow		
X	Light Yellow		
Y	Light Yellow		
Z	Light Yellow		

Colourless Gems

Danburite, Goshenite, Zircon, Sapphire and Pollucite offer gem connoisseurs a rare alternative to Diamond.

When someone mentions colourless gems to you, I bet the first image to enter your head is a Diamond! Why is this? Well it's probably to do with the fact that over the past 60 years the Diamond has been so heavily marketed, that it has become the most popular gemstone on the planet. However, it certainly is not the rarest and with over 60 million carats cut each year, with the exception of Quartz, nearly all other colourless gems are far rarer!

One of the most stunning colourless gems has to be Zircon. Just like Diamonds, Zircon has the beautiful ability to show dispersion and the visual effects caused by its double refraction can leave you speechless. What makes Zircon even more special is that many specimens were created 4.6 billion years ago, right at the time the Earth itself was formed! Goshenite the colourless Beryl is also a very attractive clear gemstone and Danburite from Connecticut, USA, looks so much like a Diamond that in Japan it is known as the Japanese Diamond. Many colourless gems are such due to a lack of impurities (see allochromatic). In addition to transparent colourless gems, there are also several opaque white gems. These include Agate, Opal, and Pearl.

is derived from the Hebrew 'goral', (a small stone used in the drawing of lots), for coral branches used to be used in oracles in Palestine, Asia Minor and around the Mediterranean".

It is important to realise that the Coral used in jewellery does not come from the beautiful and protected coral reefs in the Southern Ocean or near the Australian coast line. Coral used in jewellery is actually a bland matt colour until it is polished and treated and whilst in the past they use to be harvested by trawlers who would dredge the bottom of the sea with big nets, causing untold damage to the environment, today most coral is extracted by divers.

Essentially, Coral is calcified skeletons of sea creatures that grow in tree-like formations. Most Coral used for the production of jewellery is from the Mediterranean Sea or from the Pacific Ocean near Japan and Taiwan.

Pink Coral is a very dense and hard gemstone. Its colour runs through the entire pink spectrum, from almost white to a deep salmon shade. 'Coral' is also used as a colour, describing pinky orange hues.

Red Coral has a history pre-dating Rome, and has been highly regarded since early civilizations for its colour, lustre and texture. Red Coral and Pink Coral are usually from the coasts of France, Italy, Africa and Japan (which also has White Coral).

Golden Coral is found off the coast of Hawaii and the West Indies. Other locations for Coral include: The Red Sea, Algeria, Tunisia and Malaysia.

Sponge Coral is quite a popular form of Coral used for beaded jewellery. It is often dyed and is very porous in comparison to other forms of Coral.

As with many gemstones that are of an organic nature, Coral jewellery needs to be handled with a little more care than normal. To maintain its beauty, it is important to realize that as gems go, Coral is fairly soft, so try to avoid wearing it along side harder pieces of jewellery. It's also porous, so if you spray your perfume on it there is a chance it might be absorbed, causing discolouration to the gem.

Created Gems
A man-made item that should not be called a gem at all.

Synthetic, lab grown and created gems are all manmade and should therefore not be compared to real gemstones. As they are created by man, they are not rare and as they are not rare they should not even be called gemstones.

One thing that really annoys collectors of gemstones and those who respect the work of Mother Nature, is when people advertise manmade gems such as Cubic Zirconia and Moissanite and measure their weight with carats! This is completely misleading. These are manmade items and should only be measured in grams and ounces. However, these laboratory-made equivalents do often have the same physical, optical and chemical properties as a genuine gemstone. Nevertheless, they are still not the real thing. Plus, as they can be reproduced in any quantity, they can neither be classed as rare nor be considered to have any intrinsic value.

Another very misleading term is when companies call the glass they sell "crystal". How can a glass which starts off with no crystal structure at all and only gains one once it is blended with lead be a crystal! Yes it's beautifully coloured, buts it's not a natural crystal; it's glass!

DID YOU KNOW?

In gem terms, the crown refers to the portion of a gemstone above its girdle (its widest part). The crown acts as a lens, focusing the light, which is then reflected back by the pavilion (the portion of the gem below the girdle).

CROWN

The entrance to the Cruzeiro underground mine measures around 4ft wide by 5ft tall.

of shining mica that was extracted as a byproduct from the mine.

On the surface, the Cruzeiro Mine resembles a dormant Spanish tourist mine, rather than one that is fully operational and successfully unearthing some of the world's finest gemstones. I was puzzled why this remote mine, one that surely can't be accustomed to seeing too many visitors, was so beautifully kept; so I asked one of the owners why she kept the area so finally groomed. She explained that because the family spent so much time up in the mountains, they treated the mine like home. My next question made her laugh: "But where are the mines?" She explained how all of the mining at Cruzerio was underground. There were four large veins of pegmatite that they were following and the mine was accessed by several small tunnels all neatly concealed in the hillside.

Marcelo, the mine's geologist, gave me an in-depth explanation of the mine's history. The mine first began in the 1940s, when American explorers (known locally as bandeirantes) discovered mica in the area. Due to the mineral's ability to withstand high heat, combined with its light weight, it was used in World War II to line the fuselage of fighter planes. Further back in history, before glass was invented, mica, which can easily be separated in to thin transparent sheets, was used locally to make windows. While mining for mica they stumbled across some very interesting red and green looking minerals, but this was war time and they had no time to stop and investigate them further.

In the 1960s the first gem adventurers arrived at the mine and were amazed at the quality of gemstones left behind in the inner walls of the redundant mine shafts. Just like the neighboring Tourmaline mine at Pederneira, the Cruzerio mine is cut into the mountainside at an altitude of around 1000 feet above sea level. The main entrance to the maze of

Cruzeiro Rubellite discovered during the week of my visit.

tunnels and shafts is just four feet wide and about five feet tall. Progress for the miners below ground is slow and with the tunnels being so small only two miners flanked by a security guard can work on advancing the tunnels at a time. Using explosives, on average they can normally drive forward one metre per day, however, once they arrive at an area where the geologist believes the environment is likely to yield gemstones, the miners revert to using more delicate hand tools, and at this stage progress becomes very slow.

Often the miners will first discover Black Tourmaline (Schist). As they slowly extract the rocks surrounding the Schist, they scour every square inch for even the smallest trace of coloured Tourmaline. As soon as they discover a piece, they know there is a strong possibility of finding a lucrative gem pocket in the vicinity. Saint-Clair, the owner of the nearby Pederneira mine, had previously explained to me how if you find a small green specimen

in the mine, there is a chance that gem-quality Green Tourmaline is nearby. If you find a piece of Pink or Red Tourmaline, there is every chance that within a few metres you may find a small pocket of Rubellite. Marcelo explained that this was also the case here at the Cruzerio mine.

Whilst we were at the mine one of the generators providing power to the shafts broke, and without electricity to power the lights and to provide the pumps for the ventilation machine, we had to take a short break. Whilst we sat and admired the view across the Doce valley, Douglas (one of the owners of the mine) told us a tragic story of how his father and his uncle, who were the real bandeirantes of the mine, were tragically killed in a plane crash and how his young family had continued to run the mine ever since. My good buddy and world-renowned lapidarist Glenn Lehrer, who was accompanying me on this visit, started to explain to Douglas and myself the challenges he faced when cutting Tourmalines

red. The closer you get to a Ruby red the more the value increases. Unlike Ruby, treatment of Rubellite tends to be restricted to just heat treatment (to reduce the tone) and irradiation, making the gem far rarer than its better know counterpart. When valuing it is important to remember that you will seldom find an eye clean Rubellite and the more pure a red hue, the more likely you will find inclusions. In terms of pricing, weights over one carat increase dramatically in what I refer to as a "hockey stick" price curve.

As mentioned above, what tends to set Cruzeiro Tourmaline apart from those found in other locations is its stunning clarity. Marcelo, the mine's geologist, explained to me that this was primarily because the geological conditions where the gem was found in the Cruzeiro mine was less hostile than the growing conditions in other locations. He also explained that in terms of colour it was impossible to say whether a certain specimen was from a particular locale based on its colour, as all Tourmaline mines tend to produce Rubellite with an array of tones, but he could often spot a piece from the Cruzeiro Mine based on its clarity.

Of course, you do have to realise that in the gem industry miners, geologists and us gem hunters will always be slightly biased with our opinions. That said, I do try and keep a balanced opinion and even though I buy and sell Emeralds from all over the world, I will always have a personal preference for the clarity provided by Zambian Emerald (unless of course we uncover better in the future) and likewise I will always have a leaning towards the incredible clarity and diaphaneity offered by the Cruzeiro Rubellite.

Crystal Formation

The study of crystallography can be quite overwhelming and without first obtaining a degree in science, is difficult to grasp. Here we have tried our best to explain how crystals are formed in plain English.

First, it is important to understand that most coloured gems are also minerals (other than those which are organic such as Pearl, Coral, Amber, Jet etc).

Secondly, take it as a fact that most minerals occur as crystals.

Finally, crystals are formed when billions and billions of tiny atoms link together in a precise three-dimensional pattern that is repeated over and over again.

So how do crystals grow?

In the beginning, a few atoms start to hang about together, not on street corners, but normally in water-based solutions or molten rock in fissures and cavities. Over time, as their environment around them changes, they start to connect with each other in bigger and bigger clusters. Each new atom that joins the group must join in a precise way, and those that follow must also be identically locked in.

When other groups of crystals start to grow

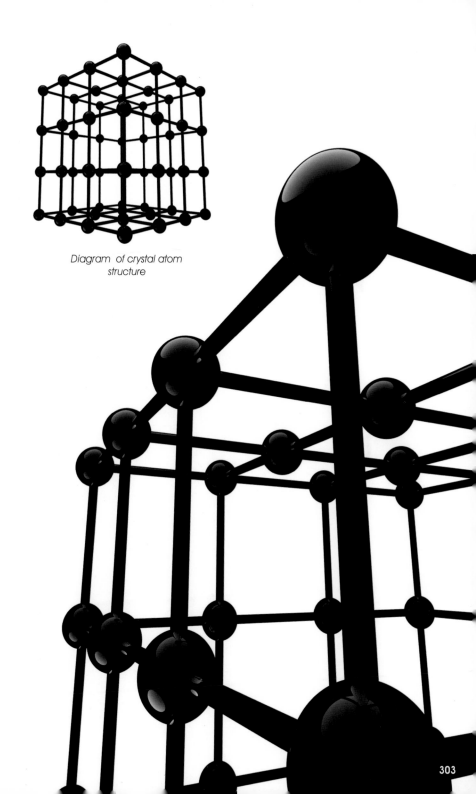

Diagram of crystal atom
structure

in the same space, they stunt each other's growth and prevent them from forming into beautiful gemstones; the net result being an igneous rock and not a valuable mineral waiting to be discovered by gem hunters.

Those rare groups that manage to keep space around them, who find themselves in the right temperature zone, those that experience just the right amount of pressure and a steady recruitment of new like-minded atoms, joining at just the right rate over a prolonged period of thousands and thousands of years, might just evolve into that one tiny fraction (approximately one hundredth billionth) of the Earth's crust that you would feel proud to wear on your finger. However, these odds diminish even further: the crystal needs to be free of major faults, it needs to be hard enough to withstand the cutting process, yet not too brittle to break. It needs to be large enough to be set into jewellery and above all it needs to be attractive. These additional factors deny the majority of the 4000 plus minerals identified to-date to obtain the "gemstone" title. As you can hopefully now appreciate, gemstones really are rare!

Interesting crystal formation inside a geode.

On the previous page you will have read how crystals are formed by the coming together of atoms. Occasionally as the crystal grows, something unusual might happen to the crystal and it forms differently to the norm. Below I have listed a few of the anomalies.

Twinning

To understand twinning, think about human twins. If they are born under normal circumstance, both can be identical at birth and grow up independently of one another. Twinned crystals are like Siamese twins, something unusual happened during their early development and they became attached. They then have to grow side by side and share the same living space.

Twinning can occur while certain minerals are forming, where their structure may be reflected, repeated incorrectly or rotated, resulting in the creation of a twin crystal.

A twinned structure will share more than one face, and the shape of the crystal might be dramatically affected or the material properties could be noticeably altered. Twinning is often due to changes in temperature or pressure during or after formation.

Twinned crystals can

often make it difficult to correctly identify a gem species. For example if a Chrysoberyl becomes twinned, its structure looks like it is a hexagonal crystal, however the actual crystal structure of a Chrysoberyl is orthorhombic. Much of the Sphene I have recently received from Pakistan is heavily twinned, which only adds to the incredible beauty of this amazing gemstone.

Polycrystalline

Crystals that are composed of many

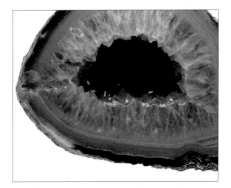

Agate has a polycrystalline structure.

crystal structures that have grown together are called polycrystalline. These gemstones are extremely durable and difficult to break.

Cryptocrystalline

Where the crystal structure is too small to be seen by the eye and a microscope is required, the crystals are known as microcrystalline or cryptocrystalline (from the Greek word 'crypto' which means 'hidden').

The biggest gemstone family, Quartz is divided into two groups: Crystalline Quartz and Cryptocrystalline Quartz.

Crystalline Quartz includes Amethyst, Citrine, Rose Quartz and Smokey Quartz, whilst Cryptocrystalline Quartz includes Chalcedony, Jasper, Carnelian, Bloodstone and Onyx.

Phantom crystals

If a crystal stops growing and later starts again, during this dormant period it is possible for other crystals that have grown alongside it to be trapped inside. This effect can often occur with Quartz. These crystals can either be very unattractive (and obviously not suitable for use in jewellery) or on the odd occasion form a real masterpiece.

Phantom crystals are hugely popular with Crystal Healers who believe that they help you put past experiences into perspective.

Chaledony is a cryptocrystalline gemstone.

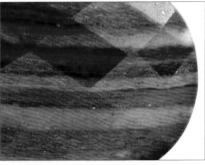

Jasper has a cryptocrystalline structure.

Since antiquity, man has believed in the healing abilities of certain gemstones. The study of the use of minerals in medicine is known as lithotherapy, and although there is no scientific proof behind any of the suggested remedies, there are still hundreds of thousands of people who believe in the mystical powers of crystal healing.

Crystal Healing (Lithotherapy)

Not only are genuine gemstones beautiful, but they are also believed to have healing power.

My own personal assistant, Barry Wiggins, who had struggled with severe back pains for many years, was once recommended to carry a piece of Snowflake Obsidian and Haematite in his pocket. I must point out that this was long before I met him and therefore is totally independent of any influence I may have had on him - in fact I only found out about his experience a couple of years ago when the topic of crystal healing was being discussed for my first book.

Barry has been carrying the gems in his pocket for many years and believes so much in their powers that he even puts them in his shorts when he goes swimming! For years, Barry has been free from back pain. Of course, it could be coincidence or it could be that there are powers that we just don't understand. One further explanation could be that Barry believes in their powers so much that it acts as a placebo.

Eminent writers throughout history, including Aristotle (384 -322BC), Pliny the Elder (23AD – 79AD) and Abbess Hildegard von Bingen (1098 – 1179AD) have documented many beliefs associated with different gemstones. Many believe that gems are linked to planets, suns and moons. Others believe that as most gemstones have taken millions of years to create, they have somehow captured powers from Mother Nature along their journey. Certain healing gems should be regularly exposed to the sun in order to recharge their powers, whereas other gems should be placed on the terrace or window sill two nights before the full moon. Some gems are said to have their powers enhanced if the gem is buried in soil overnight.

Though there is no scientific evidence that links gemstones to medical benefits, we have decided to include the following chart that we have compiled from studying the works of many crystal healers, as we believe that as long as they are not used to replace medicine and are only used in conjunction with proven remedies, then no harm can be done. After all, the power of positive thinking is known to be better for our health than having a negative outlook.

Arthritis
Gems associated with helping alleviate the pain of arthritis, although totally unproven, include: Apatite, Aquamarine, Amber, Garnet, Pyrite and Tourmaline.

Eyes
Gems associated with helping prevent and cure problems with sight, although totally unproven, include: Aquamarine, Emerald, Eye Agate, Chalcedony, Onyx and Sapphire.

Headaches
Gems associated with helping prevent and cure headaches, although totally unproven, include: Amethyst, Azurite, Diamond, Lapis Lazuli, Malachite, Moonstone, Emerald and Tiger's Eye.

Heart Ailments
Gems associated with helping blood circulation, although totally unproven, include:

Recently I had a meeting with a good friend of mine, Saint-Clair, who owns Tourmaline mines in both Brazil and Mozambique. After we had finished negotiating on a parcel of Paraiba Tourmaline he showed me a few pieces of Tourmaline with some of the purest hues I have ever seen in this highly conveted gem.

Cuprian Tourmaline

A variety of Tourmaline which exhibits breathtaking colours.

There were several different colours, all with an electric, vivid saturation. Two purple pieces, a lavender piece, several green pieces, a blue and yellow piece: all with some of the most outstanding natural colours I had ever witnessed in Tourmalines. What separates Cuprian Tourmaline from others with similar colours is that it is rich in copper (cuprian), which seems to suppress the secondary hues which are normally evident due to the fact that Tourmaline is the most pleochroic of all gemstones.

The difference between Cuprian and Paraiba Tourmaline is that to correctly earn the "Paraiba" prefix, a Tourmaline should not only have the presence of copper, but also a trace of manganese. In addition, the hues and tones of "Paraiba" should fall into a fairly narrow band of light to medium

Colour	Vivid green, pink, blue, purple and yellow
Family	Tourmaline
Hardness	7 - 7.5
SG	3.02 - 3.1
RI	1.603 - 1.655
Crystal	Trigonal
Properties	Strong pleochroism
Treatments	Not normally treated
Composition	Include copper

toned green and blue.

This small parcel was mined at Saint-Clair's mine in Mozambique which hopefully I am soon to visit. Saint-Clair explained that yields so far have been very low, just like the Paraiba that they originally went gem hunting for. Although he is not alone in searching for this gem in Mozambique, none of the artisanal miners have yet to hit pay dirt (a period where the miner starts to reap the rewards of his time, money and effort invested in mining a deposit) either.

Cuprite is a very rare gem that has the colour of a Pyrope Garnet, but a brilliance greater than that of Diamond. Both the gem's colour and its name are derived from the presence of copper ("cuprium" is Latin for Copper).

Cuprite
One of the rarest minerals on the planet.

In addition to its wonderful brilliance, the gem also has an almost metallic appearance, which for many years caused darker specimens of the gem to be often confused with Haematite.

Unfortunately almost all crystal deposits of Cuprite are too small to yield faceted gemstones. However, there was a single deposit found in the 1970s in Onganja, Southwest Africa which produced crystals both in decent size and gem-quality: a find that set the gem world alight.

Crystal Healers believe that the gem is a high energy gemstone which will help increase your levels of energy as well as helping us connect with our inner guidance. It is also claimed to help with fertility and to help release fears.

As the gem registers only 3.5 to 4 on the Mohs scale it is rarely made into jewellery. That said, using our more modern setting techniques, the next time we come across a gem quality parcel of rough we are going to attempt to mount it.

Colour	Red
Family	Cuprite
Hardness	3.5 - 4
Gravity	6.1
RI	2.84 - 2.85
Crystal	Hexoctahedral
Properties	Adamantine Lustre
Treatments	None known
Care	Careful not to scratch
Cleaning	Warm soapy water
Composition	Cu_2O

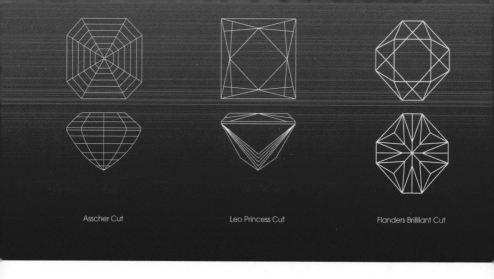

Asscher Cut   Leo Princess Cut   Flanders Brilliant Cut

Cut
A cut refers to the arrangement of facets on a gemstone.

The cut of a gemstone is extremely important, and is a key factor in determining its value. For example, a beautiful colour, eye clean clarity and a large carat weight will mean nothing if the stone is poorly cut.

The first step when cutting is to decide if the gem is principally going to sparkle or shine. Opaque gems are often cabochon cut to maximise the surface lustre (shine) and transparent gems are faceted to maximise the refraction of light from within the gem (sparkle). The reason transparent and sometimes translucent gemstones are therefore faceted is to let them effectively inhale light from the facets above the girdle, then to encourage the light to bounce off the facets below the girdle and then to exhale sparkles, and in some cases turn the incoming white light into a rainbow of colours.

The responsibility for transforming a rough gem excavated from a mine or an alluvial deposit to a valuable sparkling or shining gem lies entirely on the skills and expertise of the lapidarist.

There is a lot of confusion surrounding the meaning of cuts and many people often refer to shapes as cuts, so much so that the industry itself, in an attempt to simplify matters, or in some

Rubies can sometimes be diffused.

Coloured gemstones have undergone treatment for thousands of years. As long as the treatment is permanent, it is widely accepted that the role of enhancing Mother Nature's treasures is important for maintaining the popularity of genuine gemstones.

Diffusion
A common treatment for applying colour to or enhancing coloured gemstones.

To best understand diffusion, first of all let's remind ourselves that most gemstones are "allochromatic" (see section earlier in this volume), meaning they receive their beautiful colours through the presence of impurities. For example, Beryl is a colourless gemstone until impurities are present: iron turns the gem into an Aquamarine; chromium and vanadium turn the gem into an Emerald; and the presence of manganese creates Morganite.

One of the oldest treatments of coloured gemstones is heat treatment, whereby rough gem material is heated to extremely high temperatures in order to continue the work of Mother Nature. Virtually all Sapphire and Ruby on the market today is heat treated.

Diffusion is a technique whereby certain natural elements, those used in nature when colouring allochromatic gems, are placed on the surface of the gem during the heating process and

the colour is diffused into the gem. The treatment is permanent, however the colour created through diffusion normally only penetrates a small distance within the gem. Therefore if the gem is chipped or re-cut, the less vivid colour underneath will be visible.

One of the latest developments in diffusion treatment is from a company in India; the company is a partner of Gems TV and shares the same office complex in Jaipur as the team at GemCollector. This new technique uses thin film thermal technology to diffuse the colour deeper into the gemstone, making its beauty more resistant to chips and knocks.

The technique has just received a U.S. Patent and is widely used by many of the brands within the Gems TV portfolio. This research has also led to some amazing new colours in Topaz and Quartz and these can be recognised by the names "Spice Topaz" and "Spice Quartz".

One of the most common treatments of diffusion is with Star Sapphires and Star Rubies, where the treatment is used to enhance the beautiful asterism effect.

Beryllium treatment and cobalt treatment are other forms of diffusion. And when buying Sapphires and Rubies, unless stated otherwise, it is safe to assume that that the gem has most likely undergone some form of diffusion in order to enhance their vivid primary colours.

This is a technique used to fuse two materials together. One of its more common uses today is with **Opals**, where two are fused together to achieve more depth in the gem. While this is widely accepted in the jewellery industry, the seller should always disclose whether the gem is a doublet, as it is far less valuable than a single piece of Opal.

The doublet technique is easily identifiable in a loose gemstone where when viewed from the side you will often witness bands. It is a lot more difficult to spot in a gem which has already been set into jewellery. If you are offered a cheap Opal ring and the seller tells you that you should not get Opals wet, he is probably referring to the glue that has been used to bond the layers together!

A triplet is produced in the same way as a doublet, but has three layers. Again, when talking of Opals, it is normally the middle layer that is the genuine gem. Boulder Opal consists of fine layers of natural Opal which have formed naturally on ironstone rock: it is removed from its host rock while being cut, and placed back onto it, much like how gem-quality Ammolite is produced. For most Boulder Opals the finished gem is actually a doublet or triplet opal.

Doublet

A very common technique used to display Opals and Ammolite.

Opals can be single, doublet or triplet pieces.

Tetino Atoni in Minas Gerais, where the Dresden Diamond was said to have first been traded.

Dresden Diamond

first mined in Brazil before finding its way to India in the 19th century.

Found in the Bagagem mine in Brazil in 1857, this famous Diamond weighed in at 119.5ct before it was cut into a brilliant cut 76.5ct gem (because the current value of 1ct equating to 1/5th of a gram was only introduced in 1907, the weight of 76.5ct would have been slightly different than today's measurement).

It was named after E.H. Dresden, a London Merchant who purchased the gem in Brazil and then sold it to an English trader in Bombay (now Mumbai). His estate later sold it to Mulhar Rao, the Gaekwar of Baroda. The Gaekwar dynasty ruled the state of Baroda in Western India from the mid-18th century until 1947.

There is also the Green Dresden Diamond. It is pear cut and weighs a huge 41 carats. The gem was purchased by Fredrick Augustus in 1743 and has since been kept at the Dresden Palace in Germany.

It is said to have been mined in India and most sources seem to say it was cut by lapidarists in London. A few years back the GIA examined the Green Dresden Diamond and reported it was VSi in clarity. They stated if it was to be recut, although it would lose a few carats in weight, it would most likely then be graded as I.F. (internally flawless).

DOUBLE REFRACTION

DID YOU KNOW?

As light enters most transparent gemstones it splits into two rays, this effect is known as double refraction and can be measured on a refractometer.

with its predecessors. But when WWI broke out, people panicked. Jewellery was locked away in vaults, and much was sold to make money in order for the owner to survive.

Designs gradually started to change from the rich boldness of Nouveau to become more understated. Edward's reign was seen as elegant and sophisticated, and this was reflected in the jewellery of the period. Diamonds, a quintessential part of Edwardian jewellery, were cut into fine and delicate shapes, designed to blend in with the fragility of the lace, silk and feathers worn by Edwardian women. Many believe that Edwardian jewellery is amongst some of the finest ever fashioned. The Edwardian period's innovation is highlighted through the vast progress made in the cutting and shaping of gemstones. Many cuts and shapes created in this era were later developed and used extensively during the Art Deco movement.

Platinum was very popular and was often used to showcase the brilliance, fire and lustre of many gemstones. The metal was often 'scalloped' or had lightly engraved patterns said to resemble lace. Artisans (jewellery makers) experimented and pushed the Platinum foundries to see how it could be forged, and the result was extremely thin and light pieces of jewellery.

Another defining feature of the period was a type of setting known as 'milgrain'. It was carried out by creating a thin rim of metal, textured with tiny grains that secured the gemstone in place. This created the effect of an invisible setting, as very little metal was used to hold the gemstone in place.

A white on white colour scheme became popular, as Diamonds and Pearls were set in Platinum, creating a refined, elegant look. Elegant, lacy circle brooches, bar pins, stars and crescents became fashionable. A particular favourite was the 'negligee', a pendant that had two drops of unequal length hanging from a chain or stone.

During the Edwardian period, Princess Victoria of Wales, Princess Louise the Princess Royal and the King's wife Queen Alexandra all had a fundamental influence upon fashion and the creation of jewellery.

Today, people like to copy the fashions of the rich and famous, and the Edwardian period was no different. When the King and Queen travelled to India, Queen Alexandra was fascinated by the style and fashions of her Indian counterparts, known as Maharajas. She subsequently bought and adopted some of the styles she was fond of, bringing them back to England. Her influence started fashions for Diamond ornaments, known as 'aigrettes', Pearl necklaces with tassels, known as 'sautoirs', and the most memorable to many; chokers.

Amethyst was a favourite stone of the Queen, and because of her influence, it was common to see it used in jewellery at the time. Violet Amethyst was often used in partnership with Prasiolite

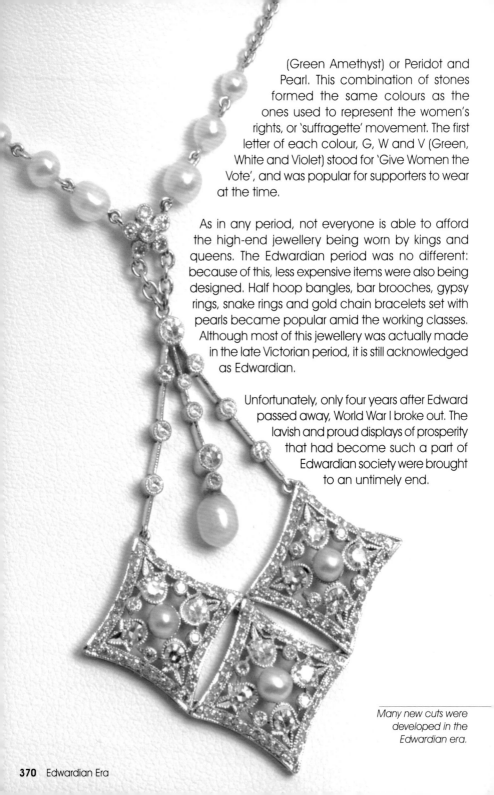

(Green Amethyst) or Peridot and Pearl. This combination of stones formed the same colours as the ones used to represent the women's rights, or 'suffragette' movement. The first letter of each colour, G, W and V (Green, White and Violet) stood for 'Give Women the Vote', and was popular for supporters to wear at the time.

As in any period, not everyone is able to afford the high-end jewellery being worn by kings and queens. The Edwardian period was no different: because of this, less expensive items were also being designed. Half hoop bangles, bar brooches, gypsy rings, snake rings and gold chain bracelets set with pearls became popular amid the working classes. Although most of this jewellery was actually made in the late Victorian period, it is still acknowledged as Edwardian.

Unfortunately, only four years after Edward passed away, World War I broke out. The lavish and proud displays of prosperity that had become such a part of Edwardian society were brought to an untimely end.

Many new cuts were developed in the Edwardian era.

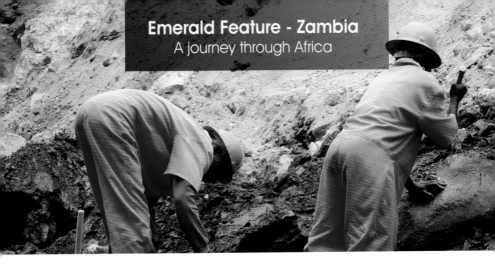

Emerald Feature - Zambia
A journey through Africa

On Sunday the 7th of November 2010 we took an evening flight from London to Johannesburg. I was travelling with my eldest son Matt who had volunteered to be the cameraman on our Emerald sourcing trip to Zambia. After 12 hours we touched down in South Africa and with just enough time to grab a coffee, we jumped on a very small plane which took us two hours back in the direction we had already travelled, landing at a small airport in the North of Zambia known as Ndola.

As we stepped off the plane I was a little apprehensive. Whilst I knew quite a lot about Zambian Emeralds, I had touched down in a country that I knew little about. All I had managed to glean from the travel guide I had bought at the last airport was that Zambia was poverty stricken - and with 1 in 7 people in the country suffering from HIV/AIDS, the life expectancy of a Zambian was a mere 40 years. The guide also warned that malaria and TB were a real issue and travellers should take every precaution possible. After

travelling for 24 hours and reading this travel overview, you will understand that I was not in high spirits.

At the airport we were met by Ian Harebottle. Ian is the CEO of a company called Gemfields, the largest Emerald mining company in Zambia. Ian is a real guru on gemstones and before joining Gemfields he was the CEO of Tanzanite One (the largest mining company for Tanzanite). Ian informed us that the trip to the mine would take around two and half hours and he started to give us some background to the country.

We were travelling through the north of the country in an area know as The Copperbelt. The area has mainly copper mines which contribute to around 70% of the nation's exports. Ian explained how the 11 million population was spread across 72 different tribes, but unlike other tribal countries I have visited in the past there was little to no friction between these different ways of life. Ian put this down to the fact that in the 1970s president Kenneth Kaunda, insisted the country should be harmonised with the national language becoming English. This made sense as until 1964 Zambia had been a British colony which was previously known as Northern Rhodesia.

Ian told us that we were travelling in an area that was very far removed from the tourist areas of the south. There, the Victoria Falls (named by the Scottish missionary and explorer David Livingstone in the 1850's after his beloved queen) attracts visitors from all over the world. To the north of the falls are numerous game parks where elephants, lions, leopards, hippos, antelopes, and even the odd fish eagle can be seen. One of the national parks, Kafue, is even bigger then the size of Belgium.

Whilst we are talking about size, geographically speaking Zambia roughly covers the same area as the UK, France and Ireland combined. The country is land locked and has one of the most interesting borders I have ever seen. To the north it neighbours The Democratic Republic of Congo, then moving clockwise it borders Tanzania, Malawi, Mozambique, Zimbabwe, Botswana, Namibia and finally Angola.

However, unlike many of it neighbours who have a treasure chest of different gemstones lying below their soil, Zambia only has Emeralds (some of the best on the planet as I discover later) and a small quantity of Amethyst and Tourmaline deposits.

As we drove along I commented to Ian how unusually green the landscape appeared for Africa. He explained that the country is situated just below the equator and above the latitude of Capricorn and that it is a very tropical country with not just an abundance of wildlife, but also a diverse range of both vegetation and fruit. The amazing thing was that we had arrived just before the rainy season had started (it normally runs from November to March) and the scenery that we were witnessing would only get better and better.

We travelled along a well-tarmaced road until we hit the town of Kitwe. From here the road turned into a very wide (almost motorway width) dirt track, with vehicles coming from all directions, bouncing up and down on the pot holes like peas on a trampoline! After another 10 or 15km, we arrived at a remote village called Kalulushi. Ian told us to prepare for an even longer, even bumpier journey from here to the Kagem Emerald mines.

What an understatement! For 35km we travelled away from Kalulushi, and the more we drove, the more the small houses along the side of the road changed from small unpainted breezed blocked abodes to mud huts with thatched roofs, with the whole hut being about half the size of an average sized UK living room.

As we travelled, I started to get a sore backside from constantly bouncing up and down in the back seat! However, as our vehicle collapsed down another pot hole and then rose above another boulder, I started to forget about the image I had conjured up after reading the travel guide. Every corner we turned people were coming out of their small dwellings and, almost without exception, they had a smile and a waving hand.

Eventually we arrived at a barrier which announced we had arrived at the mining area. To my amazement we were stopped by a very smart security guard who spoke impeccable English and who was carrying an AK47 rifle. After getting through the gate I asked Ian why the guard was carrying such a powerful weapon. In all my time visiting mines around the world I had not seen one secured by an armed gunman. Having said that, I have been held at gun point on two occasions - both by young men - once trying to take the cash that we were carrying to buy gems and another one who claimed to be a policeman who tried to take our cameras, claiming we could not film in his valley, but I digress. Ian informed me that the government

owned 25% of the Gemfields Emerald mine and they were so precious about their Emeralds that they did not want to see a single piece leaving the complex without it going through the proper routes. For this reason they had assigned several armed guards to the mine.

After another kilometre or so we came to a steel gate. This time, the security was even tighter, with more forms to fill in and barbed wire fences stretching both left and right as far the eye could see. After four security checks and what seemed like endless form filling and bag checks we finally arrived at the site.

One of Ian's team led us to the onsite accommodation. As the mine is in such a remote location, both the management and miners (some 400 or so) all live on the site from Monday to Friday. On entering our room I was delighted to find a mosquito net, spray and running water. We even had electricity until 11pm each night courtesy of a high powered generator.

After unpacking our gear and testing whether the camera equipment had survived the long and bumpy journey, we went to the miner's canteen for some dinner. The first thing that struck me was how happy everybody seemed.

They had a pool table, and those that still had energy from the full day of mining were playing a game of badminton. I spoke to one of the team and he said, "Of course we are happy, we have the best job in the world. We wake up every day with the hope of finding a beautiful Emerald in the ground and when the day is finished, we are well fed and have a roof over head. What more could a man want than dreams and comfort?"

After dinner we went to bed, covered with mosquito cream and with our mosquito nets firmly tucked in around our beds. We awoke at around 5am to the sound of heavy machinery on its way to the mining area. Our first meeting of the morning was with Ian and Gemfields head geologist Rob, who gave us an in-depth guide to the geographical area and how Emeralds were formed.

Even though Zambia is becoming world famous for its incredibly beautiful Emeralds, the vast majority of them are only unearthed in a small area no more than a couple of kilometres long, know as the Fwaya Fwaya Emerald belt. Translated from the local language into English, this means "Look Look". I can only assume this was the phrase used by the first miner in the area to unearth an Emerald. You see, with this gemstone its colour is not enhanced by any treatments whatsoever, and the first miner must have almost fainted at the natural beauty he had unknowingly unearthed.

Rob began to explain how Emeralds in the area were uniquely formed. One and a half billion years ago, a layer of earth was formed which today is known as the TMS (Talc Magmatic Schist). This layer was rich in chromium, which is the element that often turns Emerald green. Over the next billion years this TMS became covered by more layers of new rock formation. Then, 500 million years ago, molten magma started to seep through cracks and crevices in the various layers of rocks, and as the magma passed through the TMS layer it intermingled with some of its chemical elements.

The magma carried with it Feldspar, Tourmaline, Quartz but, most important of all, it was rich in Beryllium. Now Beryllium is the building block for all gemstones in the Beryl family, including Aquamarine, Morganite and most importantly of all, the King of Beryl - the Emerald. As the molten cooled at this junction where the pegmatite crosses the TMS layer, there became an environment where Emeralds had the potential to grow.

Rob and his team's job is to track these junctions and to start exploratory mining. They call these small areas, where the potential of discovering Emerald is at its highest, the reaction zones.

After the excitement had died down, CV said to me, "I have something else to show you". He walked me over to the rock face that formed the side wall of the mine and showed me an Emerald just above head height that was still embedded in the host rock.

I couldn't believe my luck. This Emerald was about an inch in diameter. After about five minutes of me taking dozens of photos and waxing lyrical to my son on film about how good luck can strike twice in a day, CV said, "We are only pulling your leg, we did not find this one this morning, but ten days ago. But as we knew you were visiting we wanted to leave it in its complete natural position, as we wanted to show it to you, little did we know we would also find Emeralds on the day you arrived!"

The gem was amazing. In the end, after it is carefully extracted with the skill of a top archaeologist, it might not weigh more than half a carat. That said, it was truly amazing. Eventually Rob had to drag me out of the mine. I just didn't want to leave - I was having an experience that dreams are made of. Rob promised me that he had a real treat in store for me. As we drove out of the pit he asked if I was impressed. "Impressed! I think I have just died and gone to heaven", I said. In my mind, Emeralds at this point had just been elevated from a gorgeous gemstone to possibly my favourite! I wish I could change my loyalty to my football team that easily!

"Come on Rob, where are we going?"

I asked. Rob started to inform me of the growing costs of having to chase the reaction zone further and further underground. He said in a few years they may need to dig to levels of 150 to 200 metres to find where the Emeralds are likely to be found. He explained that with the current open pit mine it was now necessary to excavate 12 million grams just to unearth one gram of rough Emerald, and as you go deeper that ratio obviously increases. Gemfields already spends around £150,000 a month on diesel for their JCBs and house-sized dumper trucks. These vehicles themselves are not cheap, with an annual investment of around £1.5 million needed to repair and replace them.

Entrance to the underground mine.

"So what's your solution?" I asked Rob. "We are going underground," he informed me. "We are taking all of our experience that we gained at Tanzanite One, where we had to go to a depth of hundreds of metres to find more Tanzanite, and we are going to hunt for this rare green treasure below ground." Basically speaking they had got to a depth where the costs of mining underground was expected to be less than excavating thousands and thousands of tonnes in the open pit mine.

To help with this project they hired Kevin. Kevin also played a big part in the successful Tanzanite One mine. He's a great guy who has four generations of mining in his blood. That evening, over a cold beer, Kevin explained to me how he and his wife had bought a farm in South Africa and when he retires he would like to start future generations of his family off in farming.

Back to the mine: we put on our overalls, hard hat and torch and started the long and steep trek underground. Kevin explained how one of the biggest challenges facing anyone who wants to mine underground in the Fwaya Fwaya Emerald belt is that many of the layers of rock you have to blast through are soft - especially in the rainy season when they soak up a lot of water, making them both heavy and unstable. In these areas a strong expertise in holding up your mine shaft roof is essential. Normally a comment like this as we descend down a deep mine shaft would unnerve me, but with

Kevin I knew we were in the hands of an expert miner.

Unlike many of the mines I have descended in Madagascar, where they are made of compressed sandstone, many of these layers we were travelling through were dense, tough igneous rock. I was amazed when Kevin informed me that his small team of about 10 miners were able on average to progress a metre everyday. That's amazing for a mine shaft that's around 4 metres in diameter. When I asked how well the shaft was doing in terms of yield, he only answered with a smile. As I write this diary of events on my plane journey back home, I still don't know if that meant the underground project was doing really well and he didn't want anyone to know or that they were yet to find a reaction zone that was providing sufficient gem-quality Emeralds to justify the cost.

That evening we all sat around talking about the day's events. When I got back to my room, I took out a piece of Zambian Emerald that I had purchased earlier in the year (I had taken it along to use in the filming) and started to stare at it and to really study it to a level I had never done before. I viewed it with the naked eye, I took out my 10x loupe, and I used my dichroscope. I must have spent an hour or so studying it. This was not my usual technical assessment or detailed financial valuation that I would normally carry out on a gemstone, but more of a personal "getting to know you better" type of reason I have gone into more detail than normal regarding treatments of Colombian gems, is that it's typically difficult to get a straight answer out of many suppliers in the region as to the treatments they have applied. Whenever my company creates jewellery featuring Emeralds from this area we always disclose the treatment which we believe the gem has undergone, however as it's sometimes difficult to tell exactly what enhancements have been applied we always recommend to our customers that it is safest to assume it has had one of the aforementioned treatments. We also frequently update our website with new treatments as and when the gem industry discovers/uncovers them.

Recently at the GILC (Gemstone Industry Laboratory Conference) in Arizona, I was invited to participate in a discussion chaired by Gabriel Angarita, President of the Colombian Association of Emerald Exporters, where he openly spoke of how Colombia is trying to force its traders to be more open about the treatments they apply to their Emeralds. As of yet I have not visited Colombia, so I cannot provide you with my own account of the region.

Afghanistan
Although today Afghanistan is a secondary source for Emeralds, nestled amongst huge mountains south of Asadabad in the Kunar Province are the Badel Emerald mines. These are probably the oldest gemstone mines on the planet that are still in use today and man first discovered Emerald there over one thousand years ago. I wonder if that makes it the longest continual business on the planet? Today, the quantity unearthed is very small and mining is now sporadic. A slightly more successful mining area is in the Panjshir Valley: here there are three different mining locations, but although several hundred people are said to be working the mines, we see very little evidence of this in terms of gems flowing in to the market.

When we do come across Afghan Emerald, they tend to have a vibrant saturation and a lovely, leafy green hue. One of its distinguishing features is that from certain angles you will normally see an internal whitish sheen when viewed under an intense candescent light.

Russian (Siberian) Emerald
In 2005 we purchased a rather large parcel of Siberian Emeralds. Although the tone was quite light compared to Colombian and Zambian, the gems were very open and possessed a wonderful inner life. The hue was as pure as I have seen in an Emerald. Unfortunately by 2006 we had sold every single piece from the collection and since that time I have not seen a parcel or been offered a single deal of comparable quality.

Zimbabwe Emerald
Over the past 12 months I have received three or four different requests to source Zimbabwe Emeralds. One of the reasons it is so highly sought after is that, just like the Emeralds discovered in neighbouring Zambia, the gems

are normally a vibrant green colour and don't normally need treating. Inclusions tend to be either Albite or Apatite in nature and the gems have a higher than normal chromium content, hence their very impressive saturated colour. They also have higher than normal refractive index (RI) and specific gravity (SG).

Emeralds were first discovered in Sandawana in 1956 and Modern Jewellery Magazine claimed they were "the finest Emeralds ever discovered". The mine was once owned by the huge Rio Tinto mining company and 50 years ago the mine was producing consistent volumes of pieces over 1 carat. Over the past few years there has been very little coming out of the region, but don't give up hope, as there is a lot of territory around the local mines where gemmologists believe the potential of finding quality Emeralds is high.

Zambian Emerald
Please see the detailed feature on my trip to Zambia and my discovery of Zambian Emeralds.

Emeralds from the Santa Terezinha mines in Brazil

The small, flat surfaces on the external faces of a gem are referred to as facets. When you hear someone refer to the cut of the gem, it simply means how well the facets are symmetrically balanced or how close they are to well-known standard profiles. Facets are applied to the table, crown, and pavilion of a gem and sometimes are even cut onto the girdle (the widest part of a gem).

Facets
are applied to gemstones to help enhance their brilliance.

The Tolkowsky round brilliant cut design is a cut that was carefully calculated by Marcel Tolkowsky in 1919. It has 57 facets, where all of their angles are precisely detailed, so as to maximise the brilliance and lustre of a Diamond.

On a brilliant cut gemstone, the shape of the facets are normally triangular and kite-like in appearance. On octogon and emerald cut gemstones the facets tend to be rectangular in shape. The bigger the quantity of facets applied to the crown, the higher the chance of scintillation: however, if too many facets are applied to the crown then the amount of internal brilliance seen will most likely be reduced.

Amazingly, even on a tiny 1.5mm Diamond or Topaz, often 57 miniscule facets are applied and all of the cutting is done by hand!

Pavel Sokolov - Russia
Internationally recognised gem artist

Manuj Goyal - India
Fancy cut specialist

Glenn Lehrer - USA
Award-winning lapidarist

Fancy Cut

One of the most skillful art forms on the planet is the creation of a fancy cut gem.

When the cut of a gem does not fall into one of the main categories such as a brilliant cut, an emerald cut, a cabochon, or princess cut, it is often referred to as a "Fancy Cut".

Fancy cuts are also known as "Freeform Cuts" and the GIA refer to those that have fewer than six sides when viewed from the top as "Small Freeform" shapes. As you might expect, "Large Freeform" refers to those that have more than six sides. This type of cut is often used to gain a higher yield out of the rough stone. As the skills of lapidarists increase, along with a greater understanding of how certain cuts reflect and refract light in different ways, fancy cuts are becoming more and more popular. Just like playing music or

painting, lapidary is a real art form! Just like these other art forms, there are several lapidary artists who are internationally recognised at being masters of the fancy cut; Pavel, Manuj and Glenn are amongst some of the finest talents of this rapidly growing form of art.

Please note that if you are purchasing loose fancy cut gemstones, they are unlikely to fit into standard jewellery designs and if you want to have them set, you will need to find a jeweller that makes pieces by hand.

Sphene has a greater fire than Diamond.

Fire, or dispersion, is caused when a gemstone splits white light into the seven main colours visible to the naked eye by refraction. The light disperses in the gem and reflects on its inner surfaces.

Refraction in a gemstone is caused by the change in speed as light travels from air into the gemstone. The specific properties of the gemstone slow the white light down until the different wavelengths separate into the seven colours: red, orange, yellow, green, blue, indigo and violet.

However, the human eye can only see three colours; red, blue and green. These are called additive primaries, and it's from a mixture of these three colours that the human brain can create every possible colour. It's very easy to concentrate on the physics of this phenomenon without looking at the sheer beauty and rarity. Nothing catches your attention more than a flash of colour from a Zircon or a Diamond.

Having mentioned these two gemstones, it is worth pointing out that Diamonds do not actually display the best fire possible in a gemstone. Demantoid Garnet and Sphene have a greater fire than Diamond, and Sphalerite's dispersion is three times more!

Fire (Dispersion)

You will often hear jewellers talking about the 'fire' of a gemstone, especially in Diamonds.

Sphalerite has three times more fire than Diamond.

Fire Opal

With a glow like a raging fire and a hue of a Spanish sunflower.

Unlike regular Opals, where the body colour is normally white to grey, Fire Opal is a stunning orange to yellowish-orange colour, which has a beautiful warm fiery glow. It really is one of the most unique stones in the gem world. Another name for Fire Opal is Girasol, which comes from the Spanish for sunflower.

Quality transparent Fire Opal is very rare indeed and therefore very expensive, however if you are on a tight budget and want to add one to your collection then go for a piece that is translucent to opaque: these are still very beautiful and have a glowing 'cloudy' appearance similar to Blue Moon Quartz.

Fire Opal can be found in a handful of small deposits around the world, such as Guatemala in the USA, Brazil, Canada and Turkey.

The most significant discovery of Fire Opal has been in Mexico, where it is regarded as the country's national gemstone. High up in the mountain region where extinct volcanoes shape the landscape, there are several mines now producing small quantities of Fire Opal. Most of these mines are open cast; however as the Fire Opal tends

Colour	Orange - Red
Family	Opal
Hardness	5.5 - 6.5
SG	2.15
RI	1.37 - 1.45
Crystal	Amorphous
Common Treatments	Heat Treated
Care	None
Cleaning	Warm soapy water
Composition	Hydrated Silica

you hear either term, they are simply referring to the same thing.

Over the page are a few of the species/family names are shown along with their main family members. So let us look at two examples which will hopefully make it easier to understand:

(1) Tsavorite Garnet is the variety name of a rare Green member of the Grossularite Garnet species/family, which is in turn part of the Garnet group.

(2) To slightly complicate this three-tier system, in some families/species, there are separate branches/sub species (these are not industry terms but are the best names my team and I could come up with). For example the Quartz family/ species can then be further divided into Cryptocrystalline (whose crystals are microscopic like in Chalcedony and Agate) and Crystalline sub species, such as Amethyst, Citrine, Smoky Quartz, Strawberry Quartz and Rose Quartz. But what is it that relates certain gems to others? Well, that's unfortunately not quite as straightforward! The reason why some gems are related to others depends on which families you are talking about and most families are grouped for different reasons. All members of the Quartz species/family are related due to their chemical composition being the same (SiO_2). All Beryls also share the same chemical composition $Be_3Al_2Si_6O_{18}$. Tourmalines on the other hand, all share the same crystal structure, but vary in chemical composition.

Beryl
Aquamarine
Bixbite
Emerald
Helliodor
Morganite
Yellow Beryl

Chrysoberyl
Alexandrite
Chrysolite
Yellow Chrysoberyl

Corundum
Sapphire
Padparadscha
Ruby

Spodumene
Kunzite
Hiddenite

Organic
Peral
Jet
Amber
Coral

Garnet
Almandine
Andradite
Grossular
Pyrope
Spessartine
Uvarovite

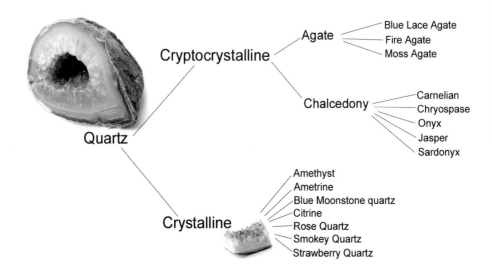

Quartz

Cryptocrystalline

Agate
— Blue Lace Agate
— Fire Agate
— Moss Agate

Chalcedony
— Carnelian
— Chryospase
— Onyx
— Jasper
— Sardonyx

Crystalline
— Amethyst
— Ametrine
— Blue Moonstone quartz
— Citrine
— Rose Quartz
— Smokey Quartz
— Strawberry Quartz

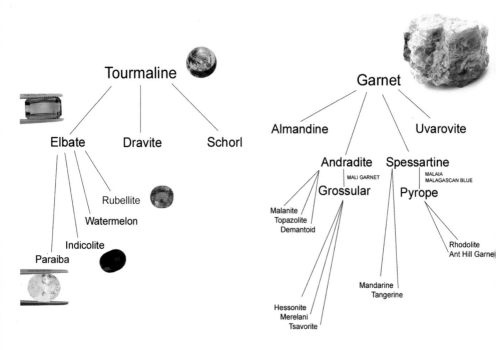

Tourmaline

Elbate   Dravite   Schorl

Rubellite

Watermelon

Indicolite

Paraiba

Garnet

Almandine   Uvarovite

Andradite   Spessartine
MALI GARNET   MALAIA
                     MALAGASCAN BLUE
Grossular   Pyrope

Malanite
Topazolite
Demantoid

Rhodolite
Ant Hill Garne

Mandarine
Tangerine

Hessonite
Merelani
Tsavorite

Ceylon), one of the best gem treasure chests in the world, is a prime source of gems created through the act of contact metamorphism. It is incredible to think that if this event had not happened, Prince Charles would not have been able to give Princess Diana her electrifying Ceylon Blue Sapphire engagement ring! Other gems that are created through this process include Garnet, Ruby and Spinel. High in the mountains of Afghanistan, Lapis Lazuli is also created in this way. Burma sits on an area rich in metamorphic rocks and much of its high quality Ruby and Jadeite are formed by contact metamorphism.

Regional Metamorphism, as its name suggests, is not confined to cracks and crevices and happens across a wider area. These rocks are often created in environments running along the edges of tectonic plates. As these plates collide with one another, the igneous rocks of each plate morph with one another under colossal pressure. As the rocks near the point of melting, and over a sustained period of millions of years, they can produce some incredibly beautiful crystal structures. As you can imagine, gems formed from the coming together of two different plates, both of which can feature many different minerals, can lead to combinations that are very specific to one area. This is, in fact, the reason why Tanzanite has only been found in one place on the planet. The morphing of two tectonic plates underneath one small area in Tanzania produced a specific cocktail that has yet to be discovered anywhere else on this planet.

Mantle Gemstones

So far, we have discussed events that happen in the Earth's crust or along its inner edge. Two gemstones however, are created deep in the Earth's mantle; Peridot and Diamond. As these are formed some 90 miles beneath the Earth's surface, and the deepest mine in the world, the East Rand gold mine in South Africa, is only 2.1 miles deep. You might wonder how these gems are discovered? Well, they are primarily brought to the surface of the Earth or near to its surface in old volcanic pipes. These are known as kimberlite pipes.

Interestingly, as Diamonds can crystallise at incredibly high temperatures in magma beneath the Earth's crust, it is believed they may be the most common crystal on the planet, however, other than those embedded in kimberlite pipes, the remainder is just impossible to reach.

Rubies are often formed by contact metamorphism.

Peridot is formed deep in Earth's mantle.

Gemstone Mining

Mining is one of the oldest industries known to man, and the "Lion Cave" Haematite Mine in Swaziland is believed to date back to 4,100 BC. According to records by Marco Polo, the Kuh-i-Lal mine in Afghanistan, which first mined gemstones in 101AD, is the oldest gem mine in the world that is still used today!

There are many different procedures and techniques used in mining: some as simple as using a pick and a shovel; some using panning techniques similar to gold panning in the Wild West; some using explosives; and others using the latest in high-tech equipment. However, regardless of the level of sophistication used, all mining commences with the exploration or 'prospecting' process. Even with an immense amount of research into this field, gem hunting today is still very much a hit and miss process.

Around the globe, gem mining happens on all levels, from entrepreneurial artisanal miners in Madagascar who often work with buckets and spades, to huge Diamond mines using the biggest machinery you have ever seen. Mining for Lapis Lazuli is done by small tribes in Afghanistan, and in the Peridot mines of the San Carlos Apache Reservation in Arizona, it is done exclusively by Apache Indians.

Gemstone mining ranges from the corporate, such as the large, sophisticated corporation that owns the Tanzanite One mine, to the more informal "pay to dig" schemes operated in some states in America (similar to "pick your own" strawberries in the UK). In Australia, there is even an underground Opal mining village at Coober Pedy! As you can see, gemstone mining is anything but standardised, and over a million people globally earn a living from trying to discover and extract the most precious of Mother Nature's creations.

Gemstones are discovered primarily in two different ways: they are either mined directly from the host rock in which they were formed, or in alluvial deposits where the gems have been separated from their host rock. Once a gem has been discovered, mines are then established either above or below ground.

Above ground (surface mining) techniques include: open pit mining, quarrying, strip mining and mountaintop removal. Underground mining techniques include: drift mining, tunnelling, shaft mining, bore hole mining, caving, room and pillar mining and retreat mining.

As I travel the world visiting our mining partners, I ensure that they mine in an ethical manner and are respectful of our environment.

An entrepreneurial artisan miner searching for Sapphire.

Gemstone Sorting
One of the most crucial jobs in any jewellery company.

One of the most difficult and time-consuming tasks when making a cluster ring or gemstone bracelet is matching the gems. Mother Nature never creates any two gemstones identically: all vary slightly in hue, tone, saturation and clarity. Before gems are set in jewellery, a massive task is undertaken by a Gem Sorter, who is responsible for making a selection of stones that are as similar as possible.

Let's assume we have an Amethyst cluster ring with 20 gems in each and that we are to make 10 pieces. Applying basic maths you would assume that we will need to sort through 200 gems. However, in jewellery terms this is not the case.

To arrive at the end result of 20 rings, all with near as perfectly matched gemstones as possible,

the Gem Sorter will have to study and compare the characteristics of possibly 500 to 1000 gems from which to make the final selections.

Without doubt, this process is one of the most skillful of all in the process of making fine quality jewellery. I have spent countless hours in my gem sorting department, questioning being applied here can be traced back to 1457.

The wardens of the goldsmiths didn't move to Goldsmiths Hall until 1748. They then started to pay a salaried assayer to test and mark items that were submitted. In 1773 silversmiths from other parts of the UK petitioned against having to send their items to London. Although there was fierce opposition from London Goldsmiths' company, an Act of Parliament was passed allowing Sheffield and Birmingham to assay precious metals.

In the same year a date symbol was added to the hallmark and was introduced to make the individual assayers accountable for their work. Every year the date symbol changed and if you have an old piece of jewellery at home, maybe a piece that has been passed down the generations, and would like to know when the piece was first made then have a look at it under a microscope and see if you can find the hallmark. Assuming it hasn't worn away, study the date symbol and then go to www.theassayoffice.co.uk and on their website you will be able to see all symbols used since 1773.

The Hallmarking Act of 1973 confirmed that all precious metals were to be assayed, and also introduced the marking for platinum.

Before 1998 it was compulsory that the hallmark comprised four pieces of information: the sponsor's mark, the metal standard mark, the assay office symbol and a date stamp. Since 1998 the date stamp has been optional.

SPONSOR'S MARK

STANDARD MARK

TRADITIONAL FINENESS MARK

BIRMINGHAM ASSAY MARK

DATE LETTER

Hallmark Symbols

Take a look at your precious metal jewellery and you may find a hallmark symbol.

The 'hall' of the word hallmark, is simply the place where the metals are tested. When hallmarks were first founded they were engraved by a mutually trusted party, or a guardian of the craft. Today the marks have to be made by a recognised 'Assay Office'.

There are four assay offices in the UK: London, Sheffield, Birmingham and Edinburgh.

Each has their own identifying symbol. London has the mark of a leopard head, Sheffield a rose, Birmingham an anchor and Edinburgh's mark is a castle. Along with the assaying office symbol and the sponsor's symbol, by law the item must be stamped with the "standard mark", denoting the level of purity of the precious metal being used. There is also an option for jewellery manufacturers to have a date symbol added to the hallmark.

It is a legal requirement to hallmark jewellery containing over 1 gram of gold, over 7.78 grams of silver or over 0.5 grams of platinum; otherwise the piece cannot legally be sold in the UK as gold, silver or platinum.

Today the forging of a hallmark is a punishable offence by up to ten years in prison, but years ago it was considered treason and punishable by death!

This cut is becoming increasingly popular for large coloured gemstones, especially when they are set into solitaire rings. Rarely used on gems below three carats, when viewed from above, the hexagon cut is similar in shape to a British fifty pence piece (I know this coin has seven sides and not six, but other than a gazebo try finding another hexagon shape that everyone is familiar with!)

Hexagon Cut

Ideal for coloured gemstones with rich, vibrant colour.

It is also worthwhile mentioning that although octagon cuts traditionally have a shape similar to an emerald cut, today some octagon cuts have sides that are equal in length, providing an appearance similar to a hexagon cut, but with two additional sides.

The shape is normally step cut, with one or two steps above the girdle and three or four below. For gems with good clarity, when studying the cut from above, it provides an attractive, symmetrical appearance and your eyes are naturally drawn along the lines of the pavilion towards the centralised culet.

The cut tends to result in a fairly large table facet (window), so it is better suited to the darker hues of gems such as Amethyst, Sapphire, Ruby, Iolite and Swiss Blue Topaz.

Hiddenite
The vibrant yet pastel green sister of Kunzite.

Along with Kunzite and Triphane, Hiddenite is a member of the Spodumene family of gemstones. The easiest way to describe the appearance of this extremely rare gem is to ask you to imagine a very lightly coloured Emerald, with good transparency and clarity.

Colour	Colourless
Family	Spodumene
Hardness	6.5 - 7
SG	3.18
RI	1.66 - 1.67
Crystal	Monoclinic
Properties	Fluoresent and Pleochroic
Treatments	Not normally treated
Care	None
Cleaning	Warm soapy water
Composition	$LiAlSi_2O_6$

It is said that the first discovery of Hiddenite was in North Carolina, America back in 1879. These first specimens were given to a geologist named William Earl Hidden who was working in the area at the time and from whom the gem's name is derived. Hidden was actually in the area being employed by Thomas Edison (the inventor of the light bulb and holder of over 1,000 patents in America) to search for Platinum. Whilst he was unsuccessful in his search for the metal, he did end up having a gemstone named after him (that must surely be better for your street cred).

After the discovery of the gem, the village nearest to the initial find was renamed 'Hiddenite' and for a period of around 10 years, the Emerald and Hiddenite Mining Company recovered a reasonable quantity of the gem. Today, the Emerald Hollow Mine located in the town of

Hiddenite is the only Emerald mine in the USA that is open to the public for prospecting, so if you ever find yourself in Carolina...! In addition to this original discovery, Hiddenite has also been found in Madagascar, Brazil and Afghanistan.

In 1882, George Kunz (possible the world's most famous gemmologist of all times and the man who discovered Kunzite - a sister gemstone to Hiddenite) wrote in a newspaper about the new discovery stating, 'the gem is always transparent, ranges from colorless [sic] (rare) to a light yellow, into a yellowish green, then into a deep yellow emerald green. Sometimes an entire crystal has a uniform green color [sic], but generally one end is yellow and the other green.'

Like Kunzite, Hiddenite has perfect cleavage making it one of the most difficult gems to cut. Due to the combination of scarcity and difficulty in cutting, most lapidarists will often not risk damaging this rare stone and therefore take the easier option of cabochon cutting this gemstone. The gem benefits from extremely strong pleochroism and slowly rocking a piece backwards and forwards will often yield several colours.

If you visit Gems TV on one of our open days then you will get to see our small gem museum. Two of the most stunning gems on display are the 365 carat Joas Hiddenite and the 242.99 carat Little Joas Hiddenite. These two are stunning: whilst very light in tone, they are both eye clean and are untreated.

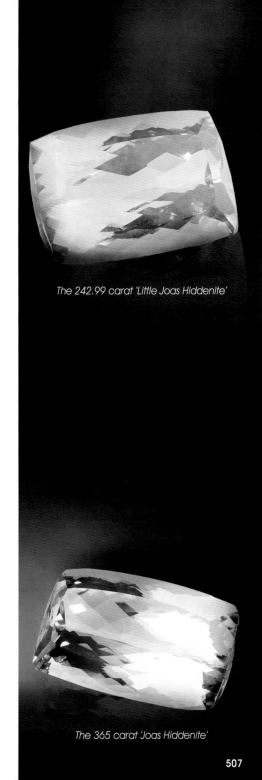

The 242.99 carat 'Little Joas Hiddenite'

The 365 carat 'Joas Hiddenite'

Hope Diamond

Probably the most famous Blue Diamond in the world.

The Hope Diamond is steeped in history. Appearing a brilliant blue to the naked eye, under ultraviolet light it looks a fluorescent red. It is currently on display in the Smithsonian Natural History museum in Washington, USA and is protected by three inches of bullet-proof glass in the Harry Winston room.

It was originally found in India as a rough crystal weighing a massive 112 carats! The history of the gem commences in 1668 with French traveller Jean Baptiste Tavernier. He was approached by a slave whilst in India, carrying what he believed to be a stunning rough cut triangular Sapphire. But Tavernier was a worldly man and realised that the slave had in his possession the rarest of Blue Diamonds.

As you can imagine, Tavernier bought this stone as quickly as he could and managed to smuggle it to Paris, where he sold it to King Louis XIV. Under Royal control, the gem was re-cut by the famous lapidarist Sieur Pitau into a round shape and became known as the "Blue Diamond of the Crown". Unfortunately, the re-cutting of the gem reduced its size to 67 carats. The king proudly had the Diamond set into a necklace, which he often wore on ceremonial occasions.

In 1791, Louis XVI and Marie Antoinette attempted to flee France. After finally doing so the government seized all of the royal jewellery; this was indeed quite befitting as the unpopular queen was believed to have been involved in the 1785 Diamond necklace scandal. During the French Revolution the entire collection was looted.

Next, the gem was said to have found its way into the possession of George IV of England; it was reported to have been sold after his death to help pay off his enormous debts.

In 1839, gem collector Henry Philip Hope, after whom it was later named, acquired it. At this point the gem had been re-cut several times and now weighed 55.2ct. Unfortunately, he died the same year he obtained the gem and after a legal dispute it eventually became the property of his nephew.

After this, it stayed in the Hope family until it was sold in the early 1900s to a London jewel merchant. It changed many hands from then until 1949 when it was sold to Harry Winston. He was then persuaded to donate the Diamond to the Smithsonian Institution on November 10th, 1958.

Between its initial find and its donation to the Smithsonian Institution, the carat weight of this amazing Diamond diminished to its current weight of 45.52 carats. In 2010 the gem was removed from the museum, extracted from its 1910 Cartier Platinum Oval setting,

and a miniscule hole was drilled into it so that scientists could analyse its composition. The gem was then set into a more modern design called 'Embracing Hope', in order to mark the 50th anniversary of its donation to the museum, as well as the 100th anniversary of the museum.

The gem is unusual in that it exhibits a red phosphorescence (a glow in the dark phenomena often witnessed in Kunzite) after being exposed to ultraviolet light. Its saturation in colour is slightly masked by a greyish tint and the GIA in 1988 certified the Hope Diamond as weighing 54.52 carats and being of a "fancy dark greyish blue" colour. In 1996 the gem was re-examined and its colour report subtly modified to a more marketable "fancy deep greyish-blue".

The earliest date that definite records began of the Hope Diamond (until this point many experts claim there is a potential that stories may relate to another Blue Diamond) is in 1812 when the gem was recorded as being in the possession of a London Diamond dealer Daniel Eliason. Interestingly this recording was exactly 20 years after the date the famous Blue Diamond was stolen from Paris, 20 years being the exact period of time when the crime could no longer be punishable. Coincidence? Probably not!

Whilst the Hope Diamond will most likely never be put up for sale again, today there are often beautiful Blue Diamond cluster rings being auctioned at Gems TV.

Howlite
One of Mother Nature's greatest imitators.

Howlite is famed for imitating other minerals, such as Turquoise. It is naturally white or grey, but due to the porous texture of the stone can very easily be dyed a Turquoise blue.

It forms in nodules that look like cauliflower heads displaying black veins throughout the gemstone, and although this mineral is not very hard it has a distinct toughness.

In its natural state, its soft, grey marble effect makes it ideal for setting as beaded necklaces or bracelets.

Its porous property makes it easy to dye, and many modern designers are producing Howlite designs featuring dyed Howlite – often emulating Turquoise.

It is said that Howlite can eliminate anger and offensive behaviour. Healers consider it an important gemstone to cleanse auras and purify the blood.

Howlite was discovered near Windsor, Nova Scotia in Canada in the late 1680s when gypsum miners came across it. As it was tougher than gypsum it was causing them problems slowing down their mining and they called in a local geologist named Henry How to help them. The gemstone was later named in his honour.

Colour	White to Grey
Family	Howlite
Hardness	3.5
SG	2.6 – 2.9
RI	1.58 – 1.61
Crystal	Monoclinic
Properties	Porous
Treatments	Sometimes dyed
Care	Be careful not to scratch
Cleaning	Warm soapy water
Composition	Complex

Due to high water table, the former mine is now a lake.

the event you get immense pleasure dreaming about it".

Mining for the rough material is made very difficult by the fact the area sits on a high water table. The mine owner explained that what looked like a normal lake to us was in fact an open pit mine a mere 8 months ago. This meant that a 40 metre deep lake had formed in 8 months due to water seeping through the ground and therefore they had started digging another open pit 100 metres away. However, the pumping that needs to be done to continually remove the water out of the open pit mine is excessive and makes mining very difficult and costly.

The scarcity of the gemstone is evident from the size of the mine. Considering this is the only area of the world where we can source Imperial Topaz, the fact that only 3 miners are digging at any one time shows the difficulty of sourcing this gemstone. Once a piece of rough is found it is handed to the security guard. After waiting around

for 2 and a half hours, we finally saw a piece of rough being brought out of the mine. Similar to mining your Zambian Emerald, a lot of rubble has to be moved to find this beautiful golden stone.

Imperial Topaz comes out of the ground in very small crystals, and to get a gem of quality and size is a rarity.

But let me tell you a little more about this wonderful, glowing gem. Of all the gemstones mentioned in the Bible, Imperial Topaz is possibly the scarcest of them all. In Ezekiel 28:13, Topaz was one of the "stones of fire" given to Moses I can think of no better way to describe the gem's sensational colour, which can vary between delicious combinations of golden yellow, rose pink, peach and sunset orange. Just like Zultanite and Rubellite, this is a gemstone whose appearance seems to change daily. Due to its pleochroism, depending on the light source, you are going to experience different hues at different times. The gem will look different at sunrise, midday and sunset. It will take on a totally different look under candlelight than it will in your kitchen under the light of your fluorescent tubes. As gem expert Jim Fiebig once said when visiting our studios in the UK, "after you have owned an Imperial Topaz for a while, you develop a relationship with it. If a friend then asks you about its colour, you will find yourself waxing lyrical about it for hours. This gem literally lives, it has a personality which is always upbeat and for this reason it is one of the most sought after gems on our planet".

As with other Topaz, the gem is normally eye clean (when you look at the gem sitting on your desk or if set in a ring with an outstretched arm, if you don't see inclusions then this is what I refer to as an eye clean gemstone). In terms of cut, due to the crystal structure of the gem it will normally be faceted into an octagon or emerald cut.

Almost without exception, as the rough material coming out of the ground is so expensive, so as to retain as much carat weight as possible it will normally be free cut and not calibrated.

Having spent time in the beautiful historic city of Ouro Preto, having seen how much work, effort, time and money is spent unearthing just a handful of pieces each day, having had Glenn Lehrer explain in depth how exciting yet frightening it is to cut such a rare treasure from our earth, I have found myself falling in love with yet another gemstone.

Whilst there is an array of splendid colours of Topaz available in the Market today, Imperial Topaz is unique in that its colour is totally natural. For those who love watching an evening sunset, there is nothing that quite competes with the colour of Imperial Topaz (with the possible exception of the equally rare Padparadascha Sapphire).

Jacque**Christie**

Jade

A stunning ornamental gemstone that is steeped in history and has been set in jewellery for thousands of years. The word 'Jade' is thought to have come from the Spanish phrase 'piedra de ijada' or 'loin stone'. When used without a prefix, 'Jade' refers to the green variety of the gemstone, and is also used as the name of a colour in its own right. It can be shaped and carved into the most intricate and beautiful designs.

Colour	Normally green, but also pastel blue, lavender, white, yellow, black and pink
Family	Jade is effectively a family, with its two siblings being Nephrite and Jadeite
Hardness	6.5 – 7
SG	3.25 – 3.35
RI	1.640 – 1.667
Crystal	Monoclinic
Properties	Vitreous lustre
Care	No specific care required
Cleaning	Ultrasonic or warm soapy water
Composition	$NaAlSi_2O_6$

In the 19th century, a French chemist determined that what people referred to as "Jade" was in fact two different gemstones: the first being Nephrite and the second being Jadeite.

Jadeite is usually opaque to translucent, and often has a luscious glass-like quality and is found in several colour variations. These include delicate pastel blue, lavender, white, yellow, black and pink. The most sought after colour would be a bewitching apple green; this colour is also known as Imperial Jade. The reason it features this enchanting colour, as with many other green gems, is due to the presence of chromium.

As it has currently only been discovered in a few places around the decidedly the lion of the exhibition. A mysterious interest appears to be attached to it, and now that so many precautions have been resorted to, and so much difficulty attends its inspection, the crowd is enormously enhanced, and the policemen at either end of the covered entrance have much trouble in restraining the struggling and impatient multitude. For some hours yesterday there were never less than a couple of hundred persons waiting their turn of admission, and yet, after all, the Diamond does not satisfy. Either from the imperfect cutting or the difficulty of placing the lights advantageously, or the immovability of the stone itself, which should be made to revolve on its axis, few catch any of the brilliant rays it reflects when viewed at a particular angle."

It wasn't just the press who were unimpressed by this huge Diamond: Queen Victoria's husband Prince Albert felt the gem lacked brilliance and ordered it to be reduced in size until it became more beautiful. The gem was cut and then re-cut and cut some more by Nottingham born lapidarist and mineralogist James Tennant. The work was carried out under Prince Albert's close attention, and even though he was reported to have paid some £8,000 for the work, which saw the gem reduced from 186ct to 105ct, he was never satisfied with its appearance!

In 1936 the gem was set into the crown of Queen Elizabeth (whom we knew as the Queen Mother); in 2002 it was seen resting on her coffin, as the Queen Mother, at 101 years of age, lay in state. Today, the gem rests in the Tower of London, although over the past 35 years various leaders from India, Afghanistan and Pakistan have claimed they are the rightful owners of this gemstone, a gem with a long and bloody history (BBC news reported that in 1976 the Pakistan Prime Minister, out of the blue, called the British Prime Minister Jim Callaghan and asked for its return).

More recently on the 29th of July 2010 the BBC wrote, "David Cameron has rejected calls for the famous Koh-i-Nur diamond, which has been part of the Crown Jewels for 150 years, to be returned to India. The diamond, which was mined in India, was seized by the East India Company in 1849 and presented to Queen Victoria. Indian politicians have long urged the 105-carat treasure's return. But asked about the issue during his trip to India, Mr Cameron said such a move would set an unworkable precedent and it was 'staying put'".

Like all of the world's famous historic Diamonds, there are many myths and legends surrounding the Koh-i-Nur. Some of these stories say it was originally discovered some 5,000 years ago and is the gem mentioned in ancient Sanskrit under the name of Syamantaka. What is quite clear is that it originated from the State of Pradesh, India, which until 1730 was said to be the only source of Diamonds in the world.

Koh-i-Nur Replica Cut

The famous Koh-i-Nur Diamond was supposedly cut from 739 carats to 105 carats in its present state.

The famous Koh-i-nur Diamond has been cut and re-cut so many times throughout history, that it's probably safe to assume that its current shape must therefore be one of the most developed gem cuts ever!

The gem is oval in shape and features a smaller than normal table facet surrounded by kite and triangular shaped facets that almost flow in curve -like patterns away from its centre. When studying the cut from the table, through the small window at the top of the gem a flower shaped pavilion can be seen which has eight petal-like shapes connecting to a flowerbud-like centre.

I love this gem cut so much, that we have invested a lot of time in reproducing the cut and our lapidarists have made us proud by creating our "Koh-i-Nur Replica Cut".

Now before you go calling up your solicitor concerned about buying a copy of a famous gemstone cut, let me save you the hassle by informing you that the cut is not patented and therefore, as long as it is made clear that it is a replica, then the Queen is not going to get upset. Anyway, as the gem weight needs to be in excess of 5ct to be really effective, then it's unlikely that your Koh-i-Nur replica cut is going to be a Diamond!

Kyanite, also referred to as Disthene, is best known for its deep, rich colours and rarity. The name is derived from the Greek word kyanos, meaning 'blue', and although it is not a birthstone, it is often associated with the zodiac signs of Aries, Taurus & Libra.

Kyanite

has the ability to rival the rich blues of Sapphire.

Whereas some in the trade call it a poor man's Sapphire, in my opinion this is often just sour grapes as they probably don't have access to faceted gem material. To me, the gem is one of the most misunderstood in the industry and I personally feel that over the next decade the gem will become one of the most sought after gems on the planet. Its clear, strong blue to bluish -green appearance has placed Kyanite in direct association with loyalty,

serenity, calmness, innovation and dreams. It is also said to be effective on the throat and third-eye chakras.

Mainly set in rings, earrings and pendants, Kyanite is an ideal gem for self-adornment. This shiny, translucent gemstone is famous for its variations in hardness which is referred to as anisotropism. This rare physical property is also known as polymorphism. Kyanite's hardness varies depending on which axis of the gem you are

Colour	Normally blue, but also green and brown
Family	Does not belong to a family
Hardness	Dual hardness of 4.5 – 7
SG	3.56 – 3.68
RI	1.71 – 1.73
Crystal	Triclinic
Properties	Strong pleochroism
Treatments	Not normally treated
Cleaning	No special care needed
Care	Warm soapy water
Composition	Al_2SiO_5

looking at. In one direction it measures 4.5 5 on the Mohs scale and on the other axis it measures 6.5 – 7.

Kyanite is actually made up of many different layers, making it easy to split this gemstone. This is known as perfect cleavage.

The combination of polymorphism and perfect cleavage makes Kyanite a particularly challenging stone to facet for lapidarists the world over. Because of this, Kyanite for many years was never cut into anything other than cabochons. More recently, as lapadarists have learnt more about this gemstone, some have been brave enough to attempt to facet it.

Occasionally, green Kyanite is found and, understandably, is known as Emerald Kyanite. Ravishing in appearance, it resembles the Zambian Emerald and is valued as a real treasure by gem collectors. In its regular blue form, it has a colour very similar to Sapphire and gems extracted from recent mines in Nepal and Tibet are comparable in appearance to the very finest Kashmir Sapphires.

Kyanite from these two remote locations is mined at high altitude. Unfortunately, the gem is incredibly rare and pieces over 3ct are almost unheard of. Whilst Kyanite is normally heavily zoned, occasionally pieces are found that are uniformed in colour from both of these locations.

This precious stone is also extracted from alluvial deposits in Brazil and the USA.

Even if you don't have a piece of Kyanite yet set in jewellery, you may actually unknowingly have a few small pieces hidden in your car, as non gem- quality Kyanite is often used in the production of spark plugs!

Volume II
GEMS TV™

Coming Soon

Letters L-Z

The Gem's Journey

Mining
We go direct to the source to find Mother Nature's most stunning creations

Sorting
We choose only the very best gemstones for use in our designs

Call Centre
We have an in-house UK call centre and warehouse, and deliver your jewellery within 2 to 3 days.

Philanthropy
Through our Colourful Life Foundation, we are funding the building of a school, an extension to a clinic and are working on a community farming project in Zambia.

On TV
By not having hundreds of expensive high street stores with huge rents and rates, our TV prices offer amazing value.